TRANSNISTRIA:

The Forgotten Cemetery

TRANSNISTRIA:

The Forgotten Cemetery

By JULIUS S. FISHER

South Brunswick
New York • Thomas Yoseloff • London

© 1969 by A. S. Barnes and Co., Inc.

Library of Congress Catalog Card Number: 68-27206

Thomas Yoseloff, Publisher
Cranbury, New Jersey 08512

Thomas Yoseloff Ltd.
108 New Bond Street
London W1Y OQX, England

SBN: 498 06773 4

Printed in the United States of America

Acknowledgment

The author gratefully acknowledges the courtesy of *Jewish Social Studies,* a journal devoted to contemporary and historical aspects of Jewish life, for their kind permission to reprint Chapter 8, the contents of which originally appeared in their issue of April, 1958.

Contents

Introduction

Transnistria was a geographic freak. A short-lived province carved out of the Ukraine, it was decreed into existence by the Rumanian dictator Ion Antonescu at the beginning of the German-Russian war in the summer of 1941. It comprised the territory between the Dniester (Nistru) and the Bug in the southernmost corner of the Ukraine. The province's total life span encompassed two years and seven months—from August 19, 1941 after the Russians had evacuated it until March 20, 1944 when the Red Army reconquered it.

Today it is an historical shadow, having vanished without a trace. But in Jewish history it is inscribed in blood and tears; it will never be forgotten. Transnistria spells horror—horror that defies description; savage, revolting acts of cruelty and bestiality; scenes of cannibalism in which one group of men torture, rob and destroy their helpless victims in cold blood. Transnistria symbolizes genocide.

The extermination of a race or a group of men, was the mission of the Germans under Hitler and the Nazi movement. They pre-planned their procedure, blueprinted the strategy, set up edifices and facilities for mass murder. Their large chemical plants prepared, after careful tests, the fastest-killing poisons; their extermination experts (Adolf Eichmann, Dieter Wisliceny, Kurt Becher, etc.) were sent from country to country to handle the "job." In their infernal work the Nazis remained true to themselves —thorough, systematic, diabolical.

The Rumanian genocide was of a different character. Ion

Antonescu, the dictator, was "a lunatic, like Mussolini and Hitler, but without the leadership qualities of the first and the iron will of the second." In vain he sought the support of the Rumanian political parties. He stood alone. Behind his grandiloquent statements and declarations there was no real power or organization. He issued his decrees for the deportation of the Jews without establishing any plan for the conduct of the mass departure. In the ensuing confusion and chaos all the demons of the netherworld were set loose. Every governor, prefect, clerk, every military and municipal officer could act according to his will or whim. And they did—with unimaginable cruelty, greed and sadism.

In grotesque imitation of their German counterparts they beat and clubbed their victims, caused them to suffocate in locked cattle wagons, and starved or worked them to death. But the Rumanians added some brutalities of their own: the marching in severest winter of men who were stripped naked or wrapped in paper; the mass rape of the daughters and wives of their victims; and as a grim climax, the burning alive of 20,000 Jews in Odessa.

Transnistria became the cemetery for more than 200,-000 Jews. Their story is little known, even to students of this period of history. This book attempts to present some details of this immense tragedy—*some* of the details; others are lost forever. The entire story will never be known.

TRANSNISTRIA:

The Forgotten Cemetery

1

Historical Background

Like all major historical events, the disaster that befell the Rumanian Jews during the period of 1940-1944 had multiple causes. It resulted from an interplay of historical, socio-economic, and political forces.

The past five centuries of Rumanian history have been sad and humiliating. No country was occupied longer or treated more cruelly by the Turks than the principalities of Wallachia and Moldavia; under the despotic rule of the Fanariots,[1] the unfortunate Rumanians were drained of their last ounce of blood. It was not until 1856 that the Congress of Paris freed from their yoke the two principalities which were to unite in 1859 to become Rumania. The Congress of Berlin (1878) finally recognized the full independence.

At the conclusion of the First World War Rumania, an ally of the Western powers, emerged with her area and population redoubled. With the annexation of Transylvania, Bukovina and Dobruja, all her territorial claims were satisfied. This relatively sudden rise from oppression to ascendancy fostered unbridled chauvinism. "Romania Romanilor" (Rumania to the Rumanians) became a national byword.

Although the treaties of Versailles, St. Germain and Neuilly assured full equality to all citizens, the minorities —comprising about one-third of the population—were regarded as "straini" (foreigners) living on sufferance.

13

Yet, because their contiguous mother-countries took deep interest in their situation and because they lived in compact blocks, the Hungarian, German and Bulgarian minorities were spared from atrocities. But those Jews who enjoyed no such protection and who lived in small groups scattered throughout cities and villages were the appropriate targets for the accumulated hostility and hatred of the dominant race. "Afara cu jidani!" (Out with the Jews) was a slogan heard and seen almost continuously. This hatred was not caused by the "otherness" of the Jew, his different religion, outlandish costume, peculiar way of life, but by economic considerations.[2]

Throughout the Middle Ages, Jews filled the economic vacuum that gaped between the nobility and their serfs. As merchants, moneylenders, craftsmen of special skill,[3] and physicians, their economic function was of paramount importance. With the dawn of the liberal era, large numbers of Rumanians—fine businessmen by nature—began to enter these occupations. As a result, keen competition frequently developed between them and the Jewish members of the middle class. This clash of economic interests was one of the main sources of anti-Semitism.[4]

After the First World War the competition became still sharper. In compliance with the peace treaties, the schools had to be open to all citizens and Jewish youth took full advantage of this opportunity.[5] The number of Jewish professionals, especially lawyers and physicians, grew phenomenally.[6] The situation was aggravated by the extreme efforts of the government to create an intellectual elite in the newly annexed territories where, during the previous regimes, the population remained on a low cultural level. Rumanian youths could now pursue their advanced studies almost without expenditure. As a result, within a decade a new generation of Rumanian intelligentsia emerged.

The tremendous surplus of professionals created a wild scramble for any job or source of income. The tension and friction between the competing strata was constantly intensifying.

These conditions explain the attitude of Rumanian university students, who had been the champions of freedom and democracy a century ago. The Universities soon became hotbeds of Jew-hatred and scenes of violence. Jewish students were beaten up; massive street demonstrations were accompanied by the smashing of windows in stores owned by Jews; and the hurling of Jews from racing trains was a daily occurrence. In 1927 the students perpetrated acts of vandalism devastating dozens of synagogues in Oradea and Cluj, tearing Torah scrolls to pieces and strewing them in the streets.

By their very nature, these movements were anti-democratic. Their objectives—the oppression and eventual annihilation of the Jews—could never be achieved in a democracy. They demanded a dictatorial system, cruel and absolutistic methods.

Despite Rumania's ugly anti-semitic record it is unlikely that the wild extremists would have risen to power had international developments not isolated the country from the West and driven it into Hitler's arms.

Here, in brief, is a summary of some of those developments.

The Post-War Situation: 1918–1930

After the conclusion of World War I, Rumania basked in her newly attained prominence and power. With Germany lying in the dust and Soviet Russia struggling for mere survival, France—Rumania's friend and patron—

was the leading power on the continent. France encouraged and supported Rumania's alliance with Czechoslovakia and Yugoslavia in the Little Entente of 1921,
an agreement attempting to forestall a resurgence of the
former Austro-Hungarian Empire.

True, Soviet Russia, in view of her claims to Bessarabia,
refused to recognize Rumania's eastern frontiers.[7] But the
Polish-Rumanian Treaty of 1921, offered a measure of
military security. And through the efforts of Foreign
Minister Nicolae Titulescu's brilliant statesmanship[8] rap-
prochement was established between Rumania and the
U.S.S.R.

Hitler's rise to power shook the delicate power equi-
librium of post-war Europe; Nazi sympathies for Hungary
elevated Hungarian revisionism—a shadow movement
heretofore—to one of the urgent international realities.

The Domestic Scene

In Greater Rumania, established after World War I,
there were three large and three smaller political parties.

The National Liberal Party, headed by the members
of the powerful Bratianu family (Ion' Vintil, and Constantin) was the power behind the throne. It represented
the vested interests, the landed aristocrats (boyars), big
industry and capital. Despite its name, it was a reactionary party. With the aid of anti-democratic electoral laws,
by manipulating the voting urns and by frequent forging
of election results, it succeeded in maintaining its sway
for nearly two decades.

The National Peasant Party (Partidul National Tar-
anesc) bitterly opposed this autocratic regime and its
Byzantine methods. Its leaders, Iuliu Maniu and Ion
Mihalache were men of great integrity. Maniu was the

idol of the Transylvania Rumanians for whose independence he had struggled for decades during the Hungarian regime. Yet, when the National Peasant Party assumed power briefly in 1920 its administration was keenly disappointing. Not one of the long-promised and overdue social, economic and administrative reforms was carried out. Corruption, disunity and resistence bordering on sabotage paralyzed the efforts of the leaders.

The Peoples Party, led by Marshal Alexandru Averescu, a hero of two wars, had no clear program. In most cases it collaborated with the Liberal Party. Its political role was rumored to have been to alternate with the Liberals whenever political exigencies demanded a change in the government.

The three lesser parties were all anti-Semitic. One was led by A. C. Cuza, a professor from the Jassy University. Another was headed by Octavian Goga, the poet. Despite their noise and agitation, both parties remained stagnant. Finally, there was the Iron Guard, a student organization founded and led by Corneliu Zelea Codreanu. Its members wore green shirts, were divided into legions, and referred to themselves as "the legionary movement." Because of its terroristic methods and the youth of its membership, the Iron Guard was generally discounted or despised for a decade.

The foregoing political structure was firmly established by 1930, when the accession of Carol II to the throne radically changed the situation.

Carol II

King Carol was a controversial figure. Those who knew him personally acknowledge his courage, energy and statesmanship.[9] But his vices outweighed his virtues.[10] After a boisterous youth[11] and a five-year exile from Rumania, he returned in June 1930 to occupy the throne. His turbulent reign provided the most dramatic decade of Rumania's recent history.

His bitter hatred of the Bratianus, whom he held responsible for his exile, precipitated the disintegration of the mighty Liberal Party. At the same time, by breaking his promise to leave his Jewish mistress, Magda Lupescu, he succeeded in alienating the National Peasant Party. Its leader, Iuliu Maniu, became his sworn enemy.

Retaining a quasi-parliamentary system, the king governed through his confidants (Alexandru Vaida-Voevod, Ion Duca, Jorge Tatarescu) for seven years. Then, at the end of 1937, the parliamentary elections mirrored dramatically the great changes that were taking place on the national and international scenes. The government for the first time failed to secure the necessary 40% of the votes.

The Nazi Subversion

As in other countries, Germany made great efforts in Rumania to subvert the democratic system and institutions.[12]

During the Nazi regime, Germany had *de facto* two foreign offices. The official one was headed by Constantin von Neurath (1932–38) followed by Joachim von Ribbentrop (1938–45). The other was the Foreign Affairs Office of the Nazi Party led by Alfred Rosenberg.

Dr. Wilhelm Fabritius, Neurath's ambassador to Bucharest, was careful not to interfere in Rumania's internal affairs,[13] but Alfred Rosenberg's envoys went their own way.[14] They set up a network of eleven intelligence offices throughout the country. Of the three that were recognized by the Rumanian authorities, the most important was the *Abwehr,* the intelligence service of the German Army.[15] The remaining eight organizations were clandestine. In their first move these organizations sought contact with the "historical" anti-Semitic parties. Schickedanz, the chief of staff of the NSDAP's (Nazional Sozialistische Deutsche Arbeiter Partei—NAZI Party) foreign office, made a number of trips to Rumania and succeeded in uniting Cuza's League of Christian-National Defense with Goga's party under the name of the Christian-National Party. But the united party made little headway. The office of the Gestapo established close connections with the Iron Guard. They taught their Rumanian disciples the spectacular Nazi methods, the propaganda techniques, the ruthless methods of killing and murder. They furnished them with money[16] and weapons.[17]

Eugen Christescu, Rumanian Chief of Secret Service was to offer the following testimony at his trial in Bucharest, 1945:

> The Gestapo worked from 1934 on in Rumania and was involved in all assassinations in this country, in that of Duca, of Calinescu and all the others. It had a tremendous influence in connection with the legionaries, it had a tremendous influence in respect to the Jilava massacre and from the investigations made at that time it became evident that the Gestapo furnished the weapons to the legionaries who executed those in Jilava. Later at the occasion of the rebellion it was established that a large portion of the weapons of the legionaries was furnished again by it (the Gestapo) . . . The Gestapo was conducted by Geisler who lived in a clandestine way until September 1940.

In the weeks preceding the parliamentary elections of 1937 the Iron Guard waged a feverish campaign. Their

propaganda appealed to a wide range of popular senti-
ments. They preached unbridled Jew-hatred in a country
that was notoriously anti-Semitic. They promised the
eradication of corruption in a land whose entire leadership, including even members of the royal family, had
been venal. In this deeply religious country—far from being anti-Christian like the Nazis in Germany—they built
village churches and chapels with their own hands, there-
by gaining the admiration of the masses as well as the
immensely powerful church.

The forces of the reactionary right therefore began to
grow dramatically and to exert real influence. In the
parliamentary elections of December 1937 the Iron Guard
emerged as the third largest political party. Instead of its
usual 2–3%, it received nearly 16% of the votes, i.e.,
500,000 votes.[18]

Another reason lay behind the spectacular success of
the Iron Guard. During the election campaign, Iuliu
Maniu committed a fatal blunder. The aged leader of
the genuinely democratic National Peasant Party, widely
venerated for his integrity, was a living contrast to the
brutal, uncivilized Codreanu. Yet, there was a common
denominator in their policies—hatred of King Carol,
whose family life had become an open scandal. During
the election campaign Maniu condescended to pay a
visit to Codreanu, who was thirty years his junior,[19] and
signed an electoral pact with him. The effects of this
move were portentous: the Iron Guard, previously despised by the people for its terrorism, was to rise to the
rank of a serious and acknowledged political party.[20]

Now all eyes turned toward the rising star—the founder
and leader of the Iron Guard, Corneliu Zelea Codreanu.
Who was this man? Rumanian sources both friendly[21] as
well as unfriendly,[22] describe him as a man possessing no

erudition, no oratorical gifts and only vague political ideas.[23] His influence on the masses was due to his "magnetic" personality. A mystic,[24] Codreanu was devoted to the cause of his country and Christianity.

The impact of Nazi Germany's sudden rise to world power, her extensive propaganda coupled with the vast amounts of available Marks was bound to stir up a Nazi movement in traditionally anti-Semitic Rumania. The movement sought a point of crystallization, it had to have a leader. Codreanu was the logical person for that role.

Codreanu was a murderer. In 1924 he killed police prefect Manciu for having testified against student rioters at their trial.[25] Brought before the Court of "Justice," Codreanu was acquitted. Now hysterical demonstrations in his honor were staged throughout the country. Thus the movement, whose credo was violence and terror, found its congenial leader.

What kind of leadership did he offer? The testimony of one of his confidants, Nicolae Maresh, offers some notion on that subject. Maresh, a friend of Marshal Presan and Marshal Antonescu, and former head of Rumania's Agricultural Syndicates, displayed a perfectly intrepid sincerity at his trial before The People's Tribunal in 1945. His probity cannot be doubted. Here, in part, is his testimony:[26]

Maresh: I was a good friend of Codreanu.
President: Did you bring about a meeting between Ion Antonescu and Codreanu?
Maresh: I told him: You are 30 years old, the Marshal is 50 and more mature. And I told him (Codreanu) that he had no program and that Antonescu would prepare one. I told him: It is very difficult to lead men (without a program). He answered: Two swords have no place in one sheath.

Later, under questioning, Maresh related that his offer to arrange a meeting between Codreanu and the King, was shrugged off with a curt refusal; Codreanu replied that he would cut his way to the king with his sword.

Codreanu's inability during his fifteen-year political career to formulate a platform, his blind jealousy that forbade others to formulate one for him, his primitive savagery that sought simple solutions to everything through violence, indicate that he could offer no real leadership. Nazi Germany's envoys—Dr. Herman Neubacher, Baron Manfred Killinger and other Nazi strategists—were the ones who, behind the facade of the glorified, inept Codreanu, were the leaders of the legionnaires.[27]

The king, whose throne was menaced by the Legionary landslide, first tried the homeopathic approach by naming an anti-Semitic government of loyal elements under the leadership of Goga and Cuza (Dec. 28, 1937). This short-lived regime inflicted a terrible blow upon the Rumanian Jews through the instrumentality of the Citizenship Revision Law of Jan. 21, 1938, which ultimately was to deprive nearly 300,000 Jews of their citizenship; it entailed the loss of their right to work and even to reside in the country.

On Feb. 10, 1938, six weeks after its formation, this cabinet fell.[28]

The Royal Dictatorship

Now a bloody drama started—the struggle for power between the king and the Iron Guard. The king had no friends. The rising tide of the Legionary movement posed a direct threat to his throne. He had to act and act quickly if he wanted to survive.

On Feb. 11, 1938 he suspended the constitution and appointed a cabinet headed by the patriarch, Miron Cristea, and composed of seven former premiers and Ion Antonescu. On Feb. 15 he prohibited all political parties; on Feb. 20 he proclaimed a new constitution investing him with dictatorial powers and establishing "The Front of National Rebirth" (Frontul Redesdeptarii Nationale) as the single party of the country. On Apr. 18 he had the leaders of the Legionnaires arrested. On May 27 Codreanu was sentenced to ten years at hard labor for treason.[29] In March 1939, following the death of Patriarch Cristea, Armand Calinescu, an iron-fisted political leader, became the premier.

After the *Anschluss* of Austria on Mar. 13, 1938, Germany had common frontier with Hungary; her influence and the menace it spelled extended directly to Rumania's western borders. On Sept. 29 the Munich Pact was signed; Czechoslovakia was sacrificed for the mirage of "peace in our time." The Little Entente—that mighty bastion of Rumania's security system—collapsed like a house of cards. "The Western Powers yielded there (in Munich) only one point, the territorial integrity assured to a country, in fact the whole of New Europe, as shaped by the Allies, went down on that day."[30]

At this juncture Carol II felt impelled to come to terms with Hitler. He decided to pay a state visit to him. In order to be able to negotiate from strength he first visited London and Paris. (Nov. 15–19, 1938). He derived but little strength from Chamberlain[31] and still less from the French. In Berlin, Hitler showed strict courtesy to the king but warned him against any common action with the western powers. Moreover, he demanded close economic cooperation between Germany and Rumania.[32] The king had no choice but to assent (Nov. 24, 1938).

Yet it took months before the foundations of this "co-operation" were laid down.

During the king's absence the Iron Guard perpetrated new acts of terror.[33] Explosives on the railway tracks endangered the train of the returning king. Now Carol decided to take extreme measures. On Nov. 30 he ordered the execution of Codreanu and 13 other leaders of the Iron Guard. This measure incensed Hitler, surely not because of its brutality, but because the impression might have been given that he had consented to the extermination of his followers. Relations between Germany and Rumania became extremely strained. The king was aware in the meantime of the far-reaching effects of economic cooperation with Germany and was in no hurry to enter it.

Yet after Hitler's liquidation of Czechoslovakia (Mar. 15, 1939), Carol could no longer hesitate. On Mar. 23, 1939 Helmuth Wohltat and Amabassador Wilhelm Fabritius on behalf of Germany, and Ion I. Bujoiu, minister of economy and Grigore Gafencu, minister for foreign affairs, representing Rumania, signed the epoch-making economic pact which opened the door to Rumania's ruthless exploitation.[34] Economic enslavement was soon followed by political subjugation.

On Aug. 23, 1939, the Ribbenthrop-Molotov Pact was signed. In September the Second World War exploded. The Blitz annihilation of Poland, the stunning military achievements of Hitler's 1940 spring offensive did not fail to impress Rumania's political leaders. With the Little Entente disintegrated, France defeated and Britain fighting for her life, Rumania stood alone between two greedy giants—the Germans and the Soviets.

In view of the critical situation, Carol called a crown council on May 29, 1940. It was decided to join the German camp. Since the situation of the western powers was hopeless, Carol argued, Germany was the sole power capable of saving Rumania from Russia's territorial aspirations. In order to defend Bessarabia the king had a belt of fortresses, the "Carol Line," erected along the eastern border of his country.

However, all of his efforts were foredoomed. In the secret clauses of the Ribbentrop-Molotov Pact, Germany declared her disinterest concerning the Bessarabian problem.[35] Russia waited patiently for her opportunity to strike. On June 23, 1940 when the western powers were paralyzed and Germany was preoccupied in the West, Molotov notified the German ambassador that his government decided to occupy Bessarabia and Bukovina. When the German reply emphasized concern for Bukovina's German minorities, Russia restricted her claim to northern Bukovina.

On June 26, Molotov handed a 24-hour ultimatum to the Rumanian ambassador demanding the surrender of this territory. The king turned to Hitler for protection. But he as well as Italy's ambassador, Chigi, advised compliance. The king had no choice but to bow. In a second note, Molotov demanded that the evacuation take place within four days. (June 28–July 1). This brutal demand was still more brutally carried into effect.

Now, events developed rapidly.[36] Here are the highlights:

June 27—The king asks Hitler to guarantee Rumania's borders.

July 4—A semi-fascist government is formed under the leadership of Ion Gigurtu. It enacted stringent anti-Jewish laws.

July 4—Rumania secedes from the League of Nations.

July 15—Hitler notifies the king of his inability to guarantee Rumania's borders unless the territorial claims of Hungary and Bulgaria are settled. (Bulgaria's claims were settled by agreement [Aug. 23]. Hungary's claims were decided by the Second Vienna Arbitration [Aug. 30]. As a result, half of Transylvania had to be ceded to Hungary—the second large territorial loss within eleven weeks.)

Carol was now paying for all his political mistakes. The enraged population held him responsible for the disasters. In his friendless despair he turned to Ion Antonescu who forced him to abdicate and leave the country in September 1940.

Antonescu's Dictatorship

As many another fascist leader, Ion Antonescu rose from prison to power.

He was not a political leader. He himself said, "I have no party, no political followers; I don't know whom to put in what position, in what department."[37] It is a widespread misconception that he was a member of the Legionnaires.[38] Although he sympathized with the rightist and extremist parties, he never was a member or a leader of any of them.[39]

He was born on June 15, 1882.[40] He advanced rapidly in his chosen military career. During the First World War, in his early thirties, he became Chief of Military Operations. After the disastrous defeat of the Rumanian Army by Gen. Mackensen, Antonescu bitterly opposed a separate peace with Germany, and advocated a last-ditch resistance within the "Triangle of Death."[41] Following the war he rose to the rank of Chief of Staff. In 1934 he created a sensation with his ruthless disclosure of the deficiencies of the Rumanian army and his demands for radical reforms. All he achieved was his demotion.[42] Three years later he appeared on the political scene as the Minister of Defense in the Goga-Cuza cabinet. He retained his position in the subsequent cabinets until Mar. 30, 1938,[43] when he withdrew for two years from active political life.

But the hectic days following the loss of Bessarabia and Transylvania swept him into the whirlpool of politics. On July 9, 1940, the king, suspicious of this dynamic man with rightist sympathies, had him imprisoned. At the intervention of Dr. Wilhelm Fabricius, the German ambassador and Herman Neubacher, the Special Envoy for Economic Affairs, he was released from jail and interned in a cloister in Bistrita.

Two months later, when the loss of Upper Transylvania revolutionized the country, the king in his desperate situation invited him to form a new cabinet. (Sept. 4, 1940). This proved to be impossible. On Sept. 7, the king abdicated in favor of his son and fled the country.[44] Antonescu assumed dictatorial power along with the rank of marshal and the pompous title, "Leader of the Country." On Sept. 14, he formed his cabinet composed of his true friend, Mihai Antonescu (no relative), along with several generals of the army and leaders of the Iron Guard. On the same day he decreed the transformation of Rumania into a "Legionary State."

"The Night of Long Knives," for which the Legionnaires hoped, had come. A period of unbridled terror ensued. Leading politicians, like Virgil Madgearu and Professor Nicholae Iorga, were murdered.[45] Pogroms raged throughout the country. In Bucharest the terror reached its climax when a number of Jews were dragged into the slaughterhouse and beheaded with the mechanical instruments used for killing cattle.[46]

A spate of Nazi decrees deprived the Jews of their rights and property.[47] But the Legionnaires took the law in their hands, expropriated Jewish firms, pillaged and plundered others. The extent of these robberies can be seen from the fact that 34-million Leis ($170,000) was found on one Legionnaire and stocks of merchandise, works of art, were piled up in the Legionnaires' greenhouses and homes.[48]

Antonescu's relations with the Legionnaires were far from happy. He was unable to control the spirits of evil he had conjured up. There were endless controversies between him and Horia Sima, the Vice Premier and head of the Iron Guard. At the end of the year there was an open break between the two. The Legionnaires decided that "things cannot go on like this," whatever that meant,[49] while Antonescu served notice to Sima that he would ask the country to choose between him and the Iron Guard.[50] In fact it was not to their country, but to Hitler that both parties later turned for a decision.

By now Rumania was entirely enslaved by the Germans. Among the first acts of the Antonescu regime was "a proposition submitted to Gen. von Tippelskierch, [The German general with whom a military convention was concluded] to the effect that a military mission be sent to Rumania."[51] On Oct. 12, 1940, two German divisions occupied the Rumanian oil fields. The number of occupying troops eventually rose to 500,000.[52] Because they came "at invitation," their maintenance was defrayed by the Rumanians. The expenses amounted to one billion leis monthly ($55,000,000), an unbearable burden on a small country.[53]

Military occupation of the country was followed by economic enslavement. A series of new corporations was established with Germans as principal shareholders. The

Solagra, Dunarea, Agromex, Prodag, Cerealcomertz monopolized the commerce and export of the entire agricultural production; the Colombia, Concordia administered the exploitation of the vast Rumanian oil-wells; the Rogifer took over the big steel plants, some of them, like the Resitza, employing 10,000 men.[54] The number of such corporations rose to nearly 700. The Germans invested but small amounts of money in them; funds needed for their operation were liberally loaned by the Bucharest banks. The loans granted to the Rogifer exceeded three billion Leis ($15,000,000). Immense quantities of all kinds of goods were constantly rolling to Germany, which was in no hurry to pay its clearing deficit.

Antonescu who sold down the river the entire economy and all of his country's natural resources, sought to cover up these treasonable concessions with self-glorification. In a survey of his three years of government, he presented detailed statistics of the expropriated Jewish properties emphasizing his own merits in having saved them for the benefit of "the national patrimony."[55] He had, in fact, transformed Rumania into an "organized colony of Hitler."[56]

In January 1941, the conflict between Antonescu and the Legionnaires led by Horia Sima reached its climax. The story, based on the common elements of various versions, seems to be this.

On Jan. 14, Antonescu visited Hitler and disclosing his inability to cooperate with the Iron Guard, asked for Hitler's consent to its liquidation. He did not receive a definite answer.[57] Ahe Iron Guard was backed by Reinhard Heydrich,[58] Chief of the RSHA, (Reich Sicherheist Haupt Abteilung—a Security Service as ruthless as the Gestapo) and Gen. Erik Hansen, Commander of the German military mission in Rumania.

On Jan. 21, Sima visited Gen. Hansen who assured him of the support of the German military forces.[59] On the following day, the Legionnaire revolution started. Days of horror followed: Antonescu's forces surrounded and defended the governmental buildings and ministries; the city at large was at the mercy of hordes of Legionnaires. The brutes proceeded methodically on the basis of a prepared plan. They broke into Jewish homes, house by house, street by street, looting and arresting the tenants. Their captives were tortured and killed or taken to a forest and machine-gunned. Pogroms were staged in all cities and towns throughout the country. The number of the victims was never established.

In these fateful hours, Hitler decided for Ion Antonescu. His will was conveyed through Gen. Hansen and Dr. Herman Neubacher, German economic envoy to Bucharest.

The following day Gen. Hansen summoned Gen. Mehedinti, a Legionnaire leader, and told him that "in view of the fact that for Germany and Rumania important military events are in the making, the preparation for which must not be interfered with under any circumstances," his previous promise for support had to be withdrawn.

Dr. Neubacher hastened to the secret headquarters of the revolutionists to notify them of Hitler's decision.[60]— a decision that spelled doom for the Iron Guard.

Within three days the revolution was suppressed; Ion Antonescu became the sole master of the country. He restored order, or a semblance of it.

But on June 22, 1941 with the outbreak of the German-Soviet war, a period started which dwarfed in extent and proportion all that had been perpetrated by the Legionnaires.

For four years Rumania's destiny was in the hands of this dictator. An impulsive and emotional man, he was not an iron-willed fanatic of the Nazi ideology. He loved his country with the devotion of a soldier, ever ready to go to war for it. He made contributions to the German war effort that were far beyond the limits of his country's capabilities,[61] sacrificing hundreds of thousands of his country's young men for the phantom of its future greatness and glory. As a victim of that same delusion, he did not hesitate to destroy vast segments of Rumanian Jewry. His talks and writings against the Jews are marked by lowest demagoguery.

Yet good and evil seem to have struggled within him. He reminds one of the medieval executioner who before delivering the blow asked his victim for forgiveness. He exempted 16,000 Czernowitz Jews from deportation and thus literally saved their lives. Three years later he was to regret this act of mercy. Yet, at his trial he asserted that but for him no Jew would have remained in Rumania. This is true. Under a purely Legionary regime, the entire Jewish population would have been deported and most of them destroyed. During Antonescu's administration "only" 300,000 Jews had to die.

Shall we be grateful to a mass murderer for not having murdered more?

2

The Catastrophe

The Massacres

Ever since the German occupation, rumors were rife in Rumania concerning a war with Soviet Russia. As early as November 1940 Gen. Constantin Pantazzi in a public speech alluded to an imminent clash with Russia.[1] In May 1941, Hitler himself disclosed to Antonescu his decision to attack Soviet Russia[2] and on June 10, Gen. Manfred Killinger revealed to him the date of the attack by pointing to the day of June 22 in a calendar lying on the desk.

On June 22, 1941, Hitler did indeed attack the Russians. The Rumanian offensive started 11 days later. The interim was used for making preparations and to create the appropriate psychological climate.

Antonescu began to prepare the necessary national atmosphere by declaring to his cabinet ministers in the first days of the war:[3]

> At the risk that some of the traditionalists among you will not understand me I am for the forced migration of the Jewish element in Bessarabia and Bukovina. They have to be thrown across the border.
>
> It is indifferent to me if *we go down as barbarians* (author's italics) in history. The Roman Empire committed series of acts of barbarism, yet it was the most magnificent political organization.
>
> A more favorable moment has never existed in our history.

You had my orders, I ask you to be inexorable. The sirup-like, nebulous, philosophical humanitarianism is entirely out of place now. Let us take advantage of this historical moment and purge the soil of Rumania and our nation of the misfortunes which were heaped upon this land in the course of the centuries . . .
I tell you there is no law! (author's italics) Therefore without any formality, entirely at your discretion, if it is necessary, shoot with machine guns!

He outlined his policies in the following words: I give way to the masses so they can massacre. I retreat in my fortress and after the massacres I restore the order.[4]

His vice premier and mentor, Mihai Antonescu, translated these principles into action. At the beginning of the war he summoned to the capital those persons selected to hold high administrative posts in the territories to be reconquered and said to them:

We find ourselves at an extremely favorable historical juncture . . . for the ethical purification of our people from elements foreign to its soul, which grow like cancer and blacken our future.
Lest we miss this unique opportunity, we *must be implacable.* (author's italics)
Should it be necessary . . . the provincial government will resort to the forced migration of the Jewish element and all foreign elements; they are to be sent beyond the border as they have nothing to look for in Bessarabia and Bukovina.[5]

Such were the directives for the future administration of North Bukovina and Bessarabia, and it was in the same spirit that the Rumanian Army issued its orders. Order No. 193-941 issued by the chief of the staff of the Fourth Army said:

The agents of the enemy work behind the front attempting to commit acts of sabotage, giving the enemy signs or information, even perpetrating acts of violence against isolated warriors.

The Jewish population participates in such actions. We ask you . . . to be *ruthless* (author's italics) with those guilty . . . [6]

These, then, were the methods to be applied in dealing with the Jews of North Bukovina and Bessarabia: barbarism, deportation and murder.

The military as well as the civilian authorities followed the directives to the letter. In the reconquered North Bukovina and Bessarabia the road of the advancing Rumanian troops was literally painted with Jewish blood. No one will ever be able to describe the horrors that took place: the mortal fear of the Jews at the imminent approach of the Rumanian "warriors;" their desperate attempts to hide or flee; their agony when detected and seized; the outcries of the wounded; the deathcries of the doomed; the screams and wails of those whose loved ones were murdered in cold blood before their eyes.

On July 3, 1941 the Rumanians launched their offensive. On the same day their troops entered Cudei, a town near the border. They were commanded by Maj. Valeriu Carp who a year earlier, while retreating before the occupying Soviet army, had ordered 36 Jews slaughtered in this town. In his sadism he had forced the Jewish soldiers to participate in the execution of their brethren. His own daughter had taken an active part in the massacre.[7] Now that he returned to the scene of his crimes he caused 450 of the 500 Jews to be murdered. The survivors were herded into a ghetto.[8]

This pattern was followed by the entire Rumanian army in the course of their advance. On July 4 they oc-

cupied the city of Storojineti. The panic-stricken Jews
were tracked down in their hideouts, 200 of them were
murdered, the rest—women separated from men—were
crowded into two ghettos.[9] In the nearby villages similar
scenes took place. In Ropcea the soldiers used the members of the Hass family as living targets for shooting
practice. A little girl member of the family remained un-
hurt and asked a soldier for a bullet. She got it. In
Iordanesti and Banila the local population staged a pogrom. The towns Stanesti, Jadova Noua, Jadova Veche
were ravaged by the military. Women were violated,
men's beards shorn and a large number of the Jews murdered. Of the 400 local Jews in Costesti and Hlinita,
only 40 remained.[10] The survivors in Banila were chased
out of town and their homes looted. After a night of
torture and terror they were driven back and closed in a
ghetto.

The craze that seized the Rumanians in these days is
reflected in the case of Dr. Salzberg, a Jewish physician
who was called to assist at the delivery of a Rumanian
woman. After he delivered the baby, he was beaten up by
the woman's father and shot at by a Rumanian officer.
Embittered, the doctor attempted suicide.[11]

In vain the Jews of Herta sought sanctuary in their
synagogue. On July 5 the pretor (county chief) ordered
100 of them seized and executed. On the same day in
Vijnita—the seat of the saintly Hager rabbinical dynasty
and a great center of Jewish life—21 Jews were slaughtered. In nearby Rostochi, all but ten were executed.[12]

The outstanding event of that black day of July 5 was
the entry of the Rumanian vanguards into the city of
Czernowitz, Bukovina's capital, with a Jewish population
of 50,000. They immediately attacked and plundered the
Jewish section, murdering hundreds of Jews. The next

morning with the arrival of the main forces, both Rumanian and German, a general massacre started. Rumanian troops aided by Maj. Otto Ohlendorf's S. S. troops[13] systematically penetrated one house after another advancing from street to street, murdering young and old, men, women and children. Within 24 hours the number of the victims rose to 2,000.[14]

The Gestapo arrested 400 of the leading Czernowitz Jews, among them the Chief Rabbi Dr. Mark. For two days the victims were subjected to endless tortures. Then the Germans set fire to the large synagogue and led Dr. Mark to the top story of the Cultural Palace so that he might see the heartbreaking spectacle. The Rabbi and the prisoners were then taken to the banks of the Pruth River and executed.[15]

Police units drove 3,000 Jews to police headquarters where the women were searched for valuables and sent home. The men were kept for five days and finally released against a ransom of 40-50 dollars per capita or the equivalent in valuables.[16]

The remainder of North Bukovina was occupied within a few days. And the slaughter continued. The number of the martyrs was: in Cosman 27, in Zoniache (Zvinioce) 130, in Rapujineti, 32.

Other military units pushed eastward in the Department (county) of Hotin. On July 2, they entered the town of Nova Sulita where they killed 800 Jews and enclosed the survivors in a ghetto. Four days later the newly appointed civilian authorities ordered 60 Jews removed from the ghetto and excuted. On the same day other Rumanian units reached the town of Edineti, the scene in days ahead of a large Jewish concentration camp. The entering Rumanian soldiers staged a bloodbath victimizing 500 Jews. The dead were tossed into three mass graves; after the burial the Jewish grave-diggers were executed.

During the next five days 12 Jews were murdered in the city of Lipcani and 40 in Lencauti. The entire Jewish population (160 persons) of Ceplauti was wiped out.

The foregoing acts of horror took place in the northern section of the Rumanian front. Similar atrocities were staged in the center.

At the beginning of July the Department of Balti and its capital city by the same name were occupied. Before this "the German-Rumanian airplanes destroyed three-fourths of the city of Balti . . . Every afternoon between 4–5 o'clock the airplanes rained incendiary bombs on the houses . . . The houses caught fire and burned like huge torches by night . . . During these days many Jews fled to the neighboring towns (Vlad, Taura-Veche, Taura-Nova) where the Rumanian-German troops looted them, violated women and girls and killed the men."[17]

Some of the atrocities in these towns were so repellent that they aroused the displeasure of even the Germans. On July 8 a unit of Rumanian soldiers met a group of 50 Jews between Taura-Veche and Nova. Having robbed them of everything, they ordered the Jews to lie face down in a swamp and shot them dead. The children were beaten to death with rifle butts. Major Ranck of the General Staff of the Ninth German Army, sent documents concerning these crimes to the Rumanian Chiefs of Staff in which he warned them that "such an attitude would tend to depreciate the prestige of the Rumanian and German armies before the public opinion of the world."

Such mentality, however, was the exception and not the rule with the German military. The developments in Balti sadly document this.

On July 9, the Ninth German army's detachments, continues President Walter, entered the city of Balti . . . The Jews, who had fled, started to return to the city, but they were interned in two ghettos which were established by the order of the German military police headed by Col. Kollner and Capt. Prast, one in the yard of the Moldova Bank, the other at a prison.

On July 11, 1941 in the evening, under the pretext of having fired on the Germans, ten Jews were taken from the ghetto and executed.

In the meantime, by the order of Capt. Prast an (administrative) committee was formed in the ghetto headed by Bernard Walter, former assistant Mayor (of the city of Balti) and president of the Chamber of Commerce. This committee was to take care of the alimentation and sanitary conditions of the lagers. (ghettos).

On July 15 at 5 P.M., the members of the committee were summoned to the German police station where Capt. Prast asked them to hand him the list of 20 communists for execution. The beasts added that if the list were not submitted, numbers of Jews, first of all the members of the committee, would be shot dead.

The committee, through its President, unhesitatingly refused to commit so low an act, whereupon Capt. Prast arrested them. After they had been searched and robbed of all—because of the prevalent insecurity people kept their valuables on them—they were escorted one by one to the yard of the Moldova Bank.

They were conducted by the guards before the eyes of the horrified members of their families and other Jews to the fence at the end of the yard . . .

At the fence the committee members were kept for half an hour during which the German soldiers tortured, ridiculed and photographed them. Then 46 other Jews were brought, picked from a group of 150 hostages imprisoned in the Bank's cellar, and they all were put on trucks. They were followed by the other Jews who tore their hair amidst prayers and wails and

threw themselves at the feet of those whom they knew
they saw for the last time.

Around 8 P.M., the trucks arrived at Slobozia Balti
. . . where there was a quarry.

Divided into groups of 15, the Jews had to dig their
graves . . . When a grave was dug the Jews were caused
to lie face down on the ground. Each of them got a
bullet in the nape of his neck. Some died instantly,
others had to call the henchmen and ask for another
bullet. The dead had to be buried by those still not
executed.

The only one who escaped with his life from this
group was Bernard Walter. Having had a large number
of friends in Rumanian circles, he was saved by the
devoted efforts of the Chief of the Rumanian police.

On July 15, by night, 20 other hostages were shot
to death under the pretext that Jews had shot at the
Germans.

Finally the German troops and the Gestapo left Balti.
Now the Jews were delivered to the mercy of a Rumanian brute, a Maj. Ion Gradu. He transferred the ghetto
into a forest near Rautel. Imprisoned in dilapidated
sheds, surrounded with barbed wire, guarded by soldiers, the Jews lived here starving and miserable. Many
of them died. Later the Rautel lager was removed to
Marculesti and from there deported to Transnistria.

The tragedy of these Balti martyrs provides only a
faint notion of what had really happened. The Jewish
population of this Department according to the 1930
census was more than 31,000. On July 17, 1941, Gen. Ion
Topor reported to the Army Headquarters that the number of Jews remaining was 3,841 plus 5,000 who were on
their way toward the city of Balti.[18] These figures show
that more than 20,000 persons were missing. Some had
left with the Russians;[19] in view of the rapid retreat of
the Soviet Army their number could not have been large.

Therefore, to say that between 17,000 and 18,000 were murdered would not be an overstatement.

In Soroca Department, Marculesti, a flourishing Jewish agricultural colony, was destroyed. Founded by the ICA (Jewish Colonization Association) it had developed into a self-sustaining colony of 2,300 Jewish farmers. On July 8, the Rumanians occupied the town, assembled the entire Jewish population, declared them as hostages and killed 18 of them, their rabbi included. There ensued a general massacre which lasted for hours. One thousand persons were murdered. The blood-crazed soldiers continued their slaughter in Floresti, Gura Kamenca, Gura Gainari. The number of victims is uncertain. In Climauti there were some 300.

On July 17 the Rumanian-German troops entered Kishinev (Chishinau) the capital of Bessarabia. Kishinev had a Jewish population of more than 50,000, headed by the aged chief-rabbi, J. L. Cirelson. During a wild slaughter, thousands upon thousands of Jews, Cirelson among them, were murdered amidst scenes of indescribable terror.[20]

By the end of July 1941 North Bukovina and Bessarabia —territories with more than 276,000 Jews—were reconquered by the Russians. The period of massacres had come to an end. Their full details will never be known. The advance of the Rumanian-German armies was so swift, the events so sudden, the horrors so paralyzing, that there was neither opportunity nor desire to commit the gruesome happenings to writing. Nor were there physical facilities for writing. The survivors of the bloodbaths, banished from their homes, were concentrated in ghettos and driven into exile in conditions that made the very thought of sending reports or keeping a diary impossible. The full story of the slaughters will never be disclosed.

The Ghettos

These massacres were but the first phase in Antonescu's policy of the total annihilation of the Jews.

He believed in Hitler and followed him with an abject servility rare even among the Nazi satellites.[21] He regarded the "solution of the Jewish problem" as an essential of his overall program.

At the Council of Ministers on December 16, 1941 he said:

> The Jewish question is being negotiated in Berlin. The Germans will take all the Jews of Europe to Russia and settle them in certain regions. But the realization (of this plan) will take time. What should we do during this interval with them? Should we be waiting for what will be decided in Berlin? Should we wait for a decision in a matter which concerns us? Shall we try to shelter them? Put them in catacombs? Throw them in the Black Sea? I don't want to know anything. Perhaps 100 of them will die, perhaps 1,000 of them will die, perhaps they all will die.[22]

These callous words typify the man who, at the times of massacres, "retires into his ivory tower," the villain who sent others to commit crimes while he contrived an elaborate alibi for himself.

The civilian and military authorities were quick to translate Antonescu's intentions into facts. The Jewish survivors of the pogroms were herded into ghettos. These ghettos were bombed-out factories, gutted houses, stables, and barns, entirely unfit for human habitation. Conditions in these lagers were deplorable.

The following terse, official communiqué gives some idea of the scope of the situation:

No. 223, July 17, 1941
Chief Pretor's Office
to
General Headquarters, Section II.

I have the honor to report:

In the course of my inspections in Balti Department on July 16 and 17 of this year I established that Division VIII sent to:

Falesti—Balti Dept.—1,546 Jews
Balti—1,235 Jews
Limbenii Noi—about 700 Jews into lagers.

According to my information Division VIII will send an additional 5,000 Jews to Balti.

There is no one to guard them.

There is no one to feed them.

I request instructions on what we should do with them.

Chief Pretor
Gen. Ion Topor

Men were driven from their homes to be shut up in lagers. Most of them were pauperized, without even the means to buy food; those who were fortunate enough to retain some valuables were unable to leave the ghetto to exchange them for food.

Instead of taking immediate measures what did the authorities do? They dallied for five days before issuing the following instructions:[23]

Wire No. 305, 22 July 1941
To the Inspectorate of the Gendarmes in Kishinev

In accordance with the order of the Under Secretary of the Ministry of Internal Affairs, the Jews in Balti, Falesti, Limbenii Noi are to be sent to work for their subsistence . . .

Gen. Ion Topor

This was the answer to the starving masses. They should work for their living. Where? When? For Whom? What type of work could be found behind the blazing front lines?

Evidently the authorities had decided to leave the hapless masses to their fate.

3

Deportation

The ghetto-dwellers were soon to be evacuated and driven eastward. Behind them remained their homes—robbed or to be robbed by the mob and the authorities—their silent synagogues, empty schools, and forsaken cemeteries. Group after group of doomed masses marched along the roads of North Bukovina and `Bessarabia. From the villages they were herded to the cities which became "points of concentration." Thence they were marchd toward the Dniester River (called *Nistru* in Rumanian) beyond which stretch the endless flatlands of the Ukraine. It was to a segment of this land, between the Dniester and Bug (known for three years as *Transnistria*) that the Jews were ultimately dispatched. The bridges that led from Bessarabia to Transnistria, became the "points of transfer" across which the Jews were "hurled out of the country."

The mass deportation was accomplished in three phases.

In June, 1941, the North Bukovina and Bessarabia Jews were ordered deported. Their evacuation was completed by the middle of November. At that time the only Jews left in these two provinces were those who were concentrated in three cities—50,000 in Czernowitz; 2,000 in Storojinetz, and 10,000 in the Kishinev ghetto.

On Oct. 8, Antonescu ordered the deportation of the Jews of these three cities as well as the Jews of South Bukovina and of Dorohoi Department. Their deportation was completed by the end of December. At the last moment, however, 20,000 Jews in Czernowitz were permitted

44

to stay. Four thousand of them were subsequently evacuated in the third wave of deportations in June, 1942.

The First Phase

The first group to be marched to the Dniester were the
Bessarabian Jews since they lived nearest to the river.

On July 8 the Gendarmerie Inspector of Bessarabia
ordered all rural Jews of that province segregated.[1] Sixteen
days later 25,000 Jews from North Bessarabia were transferred at the town of Coslar into Transnistria. The extent
of their hardships before this date is not known. Some
recorded facts, however, attest to the fact that they did,
indeed, suffer.

> The survivors of Hotin Department were . . . on their
> way maltreated by the soldiers and pre-military guards
> (teen-age urchins) . They held a rest-stop in Romancauti
> in order to rape the women and the girls.[2]

These 25,000 victims were the first to enter Transnistria.
We shall soon learn of their plight in that province.

In North Bukovina the earliest deportations took place
in Storojinetz Department. At the beginning of July, there
were three ghettos in the city of Storojinetz. The local
Jewish men were segregated in a school, the women in
an orphanage, while 2,500 Jews from surrounding villages
were herded into the synagogue. Forbidden to leave the
synagogue even to purchase food, many of these village
Jews resorted to eating grass. The police commander, Col.
Alexandrescu, frequently tortured and clubbed them.

On July 23, two weeks after their internment these
2,500 men and women were sent to North Bessarabia. On
their way they met their fellow exiles who came from

Vascauti, Bessarabia.³ The two groups merged on Aug. 4 and marched to Briceni, North Bessarabia.

On the same day 300 Jews from Storojinetz Department arrived at Attachi. This place, where a bridge across the Dniester remained undamaged by the ravages of the war, was destined to become one of the principal "points of transfer." Tens of thousands of Jews were to walk across that "bridge of sighs" to Transnistria.

But on that Aug. 4, the bridge had been closed by the Germans. Their guards told them that they would be returned to their places of origin and asked 6,000 Leis in order to hire carriages for their transportation. The Jews handed them the money. On their way back at the town of Volcineti the escorting policemen halted the carriages near a swamp, ordered the exiles to alight and drove a group of ten into the swamp where they murdered them. Terrified, the rest offered the policemen all their possessions for their lives. The police pretended to accept the offer, received 15,000 Leis and 100 pieces of gold and jewelry. Then the brutes drove all of them into the swamp, firing volley after volley at them. Between 60 to 70 of them escaped, the rest were killed.

The police authorities duly reported the heinous crime to their superiors.⁴ Gen. Topor settled the matter in one word which he affixed to the report: "Shelved."⁵

In these early days of the war Transnistria was occupied by the Germans, so that the Attachi side of the bridge was guarded by the Rumanians and the other side by the Germans. After the Germans had permitted the entry of 25,000 exiles at the town of Coslar on July 24 they abruptly changed their policies. They decided to halt the influx of Jews and to eject those already admitted—a decision that spelled untold sufferings for these 25,000 exiles. For four days after their entry they drifted aimlessly around. The only food they received was some kind of maize unsuitable for human nourishment. Then the Germans transferred them, in groups of 400-500 to former collective farms. On Aug. 2, they were brought back to the city of Moghilev. Within these few days 4,000 of them perished of hunger, exposure and the bullets of their guards. From Moghilev they were marched to the town of Scazinetz. There in good Nazi fashion the Germans selected about 1,000 old or infirm Jews, promising to send them to sanatoria and thereupon murdered the lot of them. On Aug. 5, the remaining contingent was driven to Attachi from whence 3,000 of them were to be marched back to Bessarabia. On Aug. 7, an additional 4,500 were to return to Bessarabia. But the Rumanians had closed their side of the bridge.

Now a cruel game started between the Germans and Rumanians. The Germans marched the exhausted Jews to another bridge at the town of Jampol. The Rumanians rushed troops there to block the re-entry of the Jews. The real sufferers in this game, of course, were the miserable Jews who, forced for weeks without food to wander from place to place, perished by the thousands.

Finally the Rumanians yielded. On Aug. 11, the Head Pretor's Office decreed that the Jews would have to be readmitted to Bessarabia.[6] In behavior that typified the lack of discipline and order in Rumania, the police refused to obey the decree, the Head Pretor had to repeat his instructions with the recrimination that "it is deplorable that the Commander of the police does not understand his mission (duty)."[7]

Thus after weeks of enforced marching, inhuman exertions, privation and degradation, 13,500 of the unfortunates returned to Bessarabia and were interned in the lager of the town of Vertujeni. Soroca Department. The missing 11,500 Jews had died in Transnistria.

In the meantime new masses of deportees were arriving daily in East Bessarabia. Wave after wave of deportees arrived in the vicinity of Attachi. They came from these departments: Hotin—3,340, Radauti—4,113, Storojinetz—13,862, Vijnitza Lager—1,820, Cernauti Department—15,324, a total of 38,459 persons.[8]

Lacking any plan or organization, the authorities were completely unable to handle the avalanche of uprooted masses. "The police department of Soroca has no means to procure food for them, to organize lagers for them . . . it is unable even to patrol them . . ." reported Col. Poitevin to Bucharest. When he was instructed to have the Jewish congregations provide them with food, the colonel answered: "the Jewish congregations cannot offer them food, as there are no Jewish congregations any more in existence."[9]

Another police colonel reported to Bucharest: "Among the Jews there are cases of typhus epidemic. They have no food. They complain that they haven't eaten for five or six days. There are cases of suicide and premature births."[10]

THE LAGERS

Recognizing the fact that the Jews could not be "hurled" across the Dniester, the authorities decided to set up lagers for them in Bessarabia where they would stay until their evacuation.

Following is a list of lagers in Bessarabia in the month of August, 1941:[11]

Department	Place	Number of Inmates
BALTI	Limbeni Noi	2,634
	Rascani	3,072
	Rautel	3,253

SOROCA	Vertujeni	22,969
HOTIN	Secureni	10,356
	Edineti	11,762
LAPUSHNA	Kishinev	10,400
	Total	64,446

The lagers of Fascist Europe contributed chapters of indelible shame to human history. The subhuman criminals responsible for them sought to conceal the conditions that prevailed and the acts of barbarism perpetrated in them. Rumania was the only country where official correspondence gave partial accounts of the real situation. The report of a police inspector notes:

In Edineti there are about 10,000 Jews. They live in abandoned houses in greatest filth. They have no soap, no chance to wash or disinfect themselves. Many are sick. They have hardly a chance to procure food.[12]

The report of Police Col. Manecuta summarizes the situation in Secureni:[13] "The lack of nourishment is excentric (sic.) especially the lack of bread. Many of the Jews have no money and are bound to die of hunger."
On Sept. 1 Manecuta reported:

The Jews complain that they are utterly destitute as they had been looted and whatever they still possessed they were forced to sell for food . . . They are patrolled by seven police and 50 pre-military guards . . . but the latter are given to thefts and other illegal practices . . .[14]

Eleven days later he reported on both the Edineti and Secureni lagers:

The majority of the Jews have no clothing, nothing to wrap themselves with. Most of them have been sent to the Ukraine wherefrom the Germans drove them back. Thus they lost, or were deprived of, all their possessions. They have no facilities for preparing food. There is no medicine here.[15]

Other sources give more detailed accounts on these lagers:

In Edineti over 12,000 persons live in five streets. 2,500 live in 26 peasant-houses. Most of the inmates hail from Storojinetz and its vicinity. When they had to leave they took along whatever they could carry on their backs and after weeks of aimless marching they consumed their last possessions. They did not have the 10 Leis (5¢ at that time) to buy a loaf of bread. A great many are barefooted. Many are almost naked. Although they are at the end of their strength they are forced to work. Their labor battalions are tortured and ridiculed by the guards.

In Secureni there are 10,200 persons, most of them from Hotin Department. They came from a shorter distance and were not deprived of all they had had. A number of them are able to buy food, others have no clothing.

Vertujeni is a camp of horror.[16]

Its horror was described in full at the Rumanian war criminal trials.[17]

On Sept. 8, 1941, Col. Agapie Vasile became the head of the Vertujeni lager. His predecessor Col. Al. Constantinescu describes the situation as follows: "The 22-23,000 Jews . . . could not be quartered in the small town of Vertujeni, thus they lived in an impermissible jam . . . All were crowded together, men, women, children, girls, sick in coma, pregnant women and, in addition, there was no chance of getting food."

Then the colonel describes how much these exiles had to suffer when people who had just arrived gave up their ghost, others fainted, pregnant women labored prematurely, and they all were full of lice and abcesses. Witness Gregore Nicolau, a magistrate, testified that these people lived in attics, chicken-pens, cellars, or the gutter. Lacking even the elements of hygienic measures or institutions, 50-60 persons died daily. Water was scarce, they had to wait for hours at the wells in order to get a bucket of water.

Col. Agapie robbed these Jews of their last valuables, he amassed 12 gold watches, 30-40 gold chains with precious stones, hundreds of gold coins, three or four Persian rugs and so on.

And another witness testified that Captain Burdescu was a tyrant; he beat, cursed the Jews . . . around him there was terror and fear . . . he confiscated watches and jewels from the inmates.

These criminals put the Jews to hard work, to pave the town with stones which they had to mine from the bottom of the river. According to the Rumanian war criminal testimony:

Men, women and children, weakened by hunger, were taken to satisfy the whims of these two (mentioned). Imagine a column of thousands of men with 10-15 kilograms of stones in their hands, beaten with rifle butts so as to make them run . . . naked, as they had been robbed of all, hungry, as these two (mentioned) gave them no permission to buy food . . .

And the indictment grows:

Police Sgt. Ion Oprea testified that . . . Capt. Radulescu . . . would take to his house young Jewesses who screamed and wept all night. These things recurred night after night. Capt. Buradescu would attend the orgies too and more often than not would bring Jewish girls along . . .

If there is a superlative for these nightmares, then it was to be found in the Marculesti lager.

Here is some of the account of the People's Court's Indictment:[18]

Ion Mihaescu testified that mice by thousands whisked along the streets and through the houses; the usually vast number of the flies was so annoying that they made sleep impossible. Personal effects were chewed by rats. The rainy season set in . . . the mud became intolerable. They (the Jews) were all soiled, but there was no means to get cleaned up. They remained unwashed for weeks. Then came the cold, but there was no wood (for heating) available. The Jews gave a watch for a loaf of bread.

Mihaescu, a high official of the Rumanian National Bank, was delegated to purchase at the official rate the jewels and precious metals of the Jews. The methods he used in this transaction are related by St. Dragomirescu, a jeweler, who served as his expert.

When I arrived in Marculesti, the misery I found there defies description. All over, in cellars, trenches, yards, lay corpses of the deportees. There I found Mihaescu who was constantly moving around and beating up whomever he met for no reason whatsoever. His bestiality was that of the worst man (sic). He confiscated the identification papers shouting: "You all are going to die!" He stole even the blankets if they were not too heavy.

He ignored my appraisals; he paid ridiculous prices to the owners. After two days my work was stopped. Mihaescu decided to take the valuables for nothing.

On his own initiative he confiscated the beds, stoves, soap, coffee, etc. of the refugees.

And the testimony of another Rumanian adds to the portrait of blind cruelty:

I was in Marculesti for two days. There I met Mihaescu, a beast with human face . . . It was his pasttime to beat people for no reason under the pretext of a search; my mother was undressed and so horribly beaten that she died within a few days.[19]

On Oct. 8, 1941, the sadistic commanders of the Vertujeni lager, Col. Agapie and Buradescu were transferred to Marculesti. Now the terror reached new heights. They, too, clubbed everyone within their reach. They robbed their victims by tearing earrings out of ears, wrenching fingers while forcing off a ring. They forbade the inmates to buy food. Those who were caught doing so were savagely punished.

The lager of Marculesti served as a clearing center from whence Jews were sent to the various "points of transfer" to Transnistria. Those who survived its horrors left it possessing nothing beyond the clothing on their backs.

The conditions in the Kishinev ghetto did not differ from those in the other lagers.

Kishinev was the capital of Bessarabia, a province that had often changed hands during its history. In the early 1900's it was annexed to Tzarist Russia. After the First World War it was annexed to Rumania. Twenty years later under the Molotov-Ribbentrop pact it was returned to Soviet Russia.

Despite all these vicissitudes, the Jewish community of Kishinev grew and flourished. In 1940 it numbered 50,603 persons. A large center of Jewish life and lore, it was headed by the aged Chief Rabbi J. L. Tzirelson, a world-renowned scholar and author, and a member for years of the Rumanian Senate where he fought courageously and resolutely against the front of the anti-Semites.

On July 17, 1941, this thriving community was devastated by a bloodbath staged by German-Rumanian troops. After seven terror-filled days, the survivors—10,311 in number—were evacuated from their homes and with whatever they could carry on their shoulders they were concentrated in a square. From there they were herded into a ghetto where 20 to 40 persons were jammed into each room of a cluster of bombed-out houses.

They were not permitted to leave the ghetto even to obtain food. They were robbed by the soldiers and their officers. One Capt I. Paraschivescu, during the 15 days of his assignment to the ghetto, hoarded in his house a veritable bazaar of oriental rugs, sets of china, etc.

The lives of the Jews were at the mercy of their oppressors. The aforementioned Committee of Inquiry established that during the second week of their internment (Aug. 1) a German officer required 250 men and 200 women for a job. Of the men, he selected those with high education; of the women, he chose—with the aid of his monocle—those of beauty. In the evening of the same day 39 men returned with the information that all had been murdered. Jews from the ghetto were sent to cover their graves with earth. A week later a Rumanian road inspector took 500 Jews for work; 200 came back exhausted and crippled, the others were never again heard of.

In glaring contrast to their persecutors' depravity stands the heroism of the Jewish victims. A lawyer, Shapiro, (his first name unmentioned) had the amazing ingenuity to obtain and wear an army officer's uniform. He flew in a

military airplane to Bucharest in an effort to save his
brethren from deportation. His efforts, however, were
unsuccessful. By remaining in the capital he could have
saved his own life. Instead, he returned to Kishinev to
perish along with thousands of his people.

RELIEF EFFORTS

On Aug. 21, six weeks after the beginning of the deportations, Dr. William Filderman, the president of the
federation of the Jewish communities, requested the Vice
Premier's permission to transmit 300,000 Leis on behalf
of the Jassy Jews and 200,000 on the part of his organization to the deportees in the lagers. After long delay the
Government issued the permit on the condition that all
money accounts must be sent to the military authorities
in charge of the lagers. The Jassy Jewish Community sent
300,000 Leis to Col. Agapie, the Commander of the Vertujeni lager. This brute embezzled the whole amount.[21] The
first relief effort thus failed completely.

EXPULSON TO TRANSNISTRIA
SEPT. 12-NOV. 10, 1941

For nearly two months the Jews were kept in the lagers
in Bessarabia.

In the meantime Hitler agreed that the territory between the Dniester and the Bug should be ceded to the
Rumanians. On Aug. 19, 1941 Antonescu's decree created
the new province, Transnistria, and annexed it to Rumania. Now the situation was ripe for the removal of the
Jews from Bessarabia.

Immediately a census was held that showed 54,028 Jews
in the lagers. On Sept. 2, the Head Pretor Gen. Ion Topor

sent the following coded wire to the police headquarters Legion in Tighina:

> I fixed the following points of transfer: from Cruiuleni to Karantia and from Rezina to Ribnita. Fix the itinerary, direct the platoons and police so that on Sept. 6, the transfer should start. Have carriages ready for requisition at the points of transfer for the transportation of the baggage, women and sick.[22]

The following day Police Inspector Brosteanu acknowledged receipt of the order in a wire to Gen. Topor:

> Pursuant to Marshall Antonescu's decision in connection with the Governor of Transnistria (sic) concerning the transport of *those known* (author's italics) on the 15th. Itinerary, rest stops and points of night quarters will be forwarded. Col. Brosteanu.[23]

The secrecy surrounding these communications is characteristic. Even in this heyday of Nazi victories, these criminals seemed afraid to assume responsibility for these measures.

Losing no time, the Chief Police Inspector of Bessarabia issued instructions concerning the evacuation of the 22,000 odd deportees of the Vertujeni lager. He set Sept. 12 as the day for beginning the evacuation. Every second day 1,600 persons should leave, he ordered, half of them be marched northward to Cosauti, the other half southward to Rezina. Thirty kilometers—approximately 20 miles—had to be covered a day. Every group should have 50 carriages for the transportation of the women and the sick. The looting of the deportees should be punished by death.[24]

These instructions were largely disregarded. The evacuations were carried out in a barbarous manner. Members of the same family were separated into different groups. In cases, where one group was marched north and the other south, they never met. The scenes at their separation were heart-rending. Men and women exhausted by two months of starvation and sufferings were forced to march 30 kilometers a day. Instead of 50 carriages, there were only five or six, for which they had to pay.

Clubbed and kicked by the police, they marched, drawing on the last reserves of their strength. The sick and infirm, unable to walk, were executed. They were buried in mass graves with a capacity for 100 corpses, which were dug in advance at intervals of 10 kilometers. The peasants lay in wait in the cornfields to loot the bodies after the execution.[25] Frequently the native population attacked the miserable crowd of deportees robbing them of their last possession.

The route to Cosauti was the scene of unbelievable depredations. An escorting policeman or pre-military youth would often sell a Jew to a peasant, for a price of 1,000–1,500 ($7-10); the police would kill the Jew and the peasant would take the clothing.

The evacuation from Vertujeni took several weeks. In the meantime those awaiting their turn were subjected to hard labor. They had to pave streets with tombstones from the Jewish cemetery, to repair roads with stones from the Dniester. On Rosh Hashona (Sept. 21, 1941) the rabbis were singled out to work in the labor gang.

The columns that took the southwest route crossed the Dniester at Ribnita and having entered Transnistria were marched to Birzula, Grozdovca, Balta and Barsad. Those marched in the northern direction crossed the Dniester at Iampol and were taken to Grijopol and then to Obodovca near the Bug.

The same methods were employed in evacuating the

other camps. The Secureni lager was divided into two sections for two routes of departure with the same brutal breaking up of families. Prior to their departure the exiles had to lie on the ground for a thorough search—and looting—of the last bits of their possessions. Half of the lager population was taken through Attachi to Moghilev, the others had to pass through the hell of Marculesti.

Because of the outbreak of a typhus epidemic the Edineti lager was evacuated a month later, starting on Oct. 11, 1941. They too were marched in two directions through Attachi and through Marculesti.

The horrors of these evacuations appalled even some of the henchmen. The Commission of Inquiry delegated by Ion Antonescu in December, 1941 reported that between Secureni and Cosauti alone about 500 Jews were executed because they lagged behind during the march.

From the statements of St. Augustine Rosca (who was in charge of the evacuations from Edineti and Secureni) it became clear that the enforcement of these orders led to such dramatic moments that those who took part in it will long labor under these impressions.

The Second Phase
October 1941—December 1941

Ion Antonescu was soon to bear down on another segment of the country's Jewry. On Oct. 6, 1941, at the Council of Ministers he declared:

Concerning the Jews I took measures with a view to their definite and total removal from these regions. The measures are being enforced. In addition we have 10,000 Jews in Bessarabia who within a few days will be transferred beyond the Dniester and, conditions permitting, beyond the Ural . . .[27]

He did not exaggerate. Two days earlier the Army General Headquarters had sent the following order to Czernowitz:

Pursuant to Marshal Antonescu's order all Jews of Bukovina shall be sent within ten days beyond the Dniester. Send report on the enforcement by tomorrow 20 hours.
Chief of Section II
Lt. Col. R. Dinulescu

Antonescu's decision was to spell doom for more than 100,000 Jews living in North and South Bukovina and in the Dorohoi Department. North Bukovina had already been Judenrein except for 2,000 Jews in Storojineti and 45,000-50,000 in Cernowitz. There were 23,844 Jews in South Bukovina. And in Dorohoi Department, an area that had been annexed to Bukovina in 1938, there were 14,784 Jews who would be affected by the expulsion decree. Adding the 10,000 Jews of Kishinev, between 95,000-100,000 Jews were affected.

These deportations were more carefully prepared than those of the summer as far as the looting of the Jews was concerned. The other features remained unchanged: secrecy about the operations, Blitz like speed in the enforcement, and the complete despoliation of the victims.

PRELIMINARIES

Economic measures

On Oct. 5, 1941 the following instructions were wired to the Governors of the affected provinces:

Hughes, Secret.

To the Governors of Bukovina and of Bessarabia.

In agreement with the National Bank, Marshal Antonescu decrees that the exchange of the jewels and precious stones of the Jews who are to be evacuated from Bukovina and Bessarabia shall take place according to these rules.

The valuables shall be paid for at the official rate in Kassenschein, or in rubles but by no means in Leis.

The exchange shall be controlled by trustworthy elements and any abuse shall be avoided.

All measures shall be taken to prevent the private sales of these valuables, their burying in the ground or destruction.

These measures shall be taken before the departure of the Jews from the lagers and at the points of transfer to Ukraine.

At the same time it is compulsory that the Leis be exchanged in Kassenschein.

The Chief of the Military Cabinet
Col. R. Davidescu

Five days later the Ministry of Finances issued its own regulations. Here is the text thereof.

The Ministry of Finances
to the
National Bank of Rumania.

In the matter of the exchange of the valuables of the Jews to be evacuated . . . I have the honor to make it known that the Ministry of Finances agrees that the rate of the ruble shall be 40 Leis equal 1 ruble.

. . . Gold will be paid for according to its weight and grade at the official rate of the National Bank.

Precious stones and valuables will be paid for on the basis of the evaluation of experts and at only 20% of the appraisal. This will be the equivalent of the proportion of the price of gold at at official rate of its market price.

You are requested to see to it that the receipts for the deposits in rubles shall be withdrawn before the departure of the Jews in this category.

Also we request you to take all measures to prevent any abuse on the part of the official agencies which will handle these matters.

For the Minister, Constantine Pandele

In addition to the confiscation of four-fifths of the valuables, the fixing of the rate of the ruble at 40 Leis was another measure of robbery. It marked the third compulsory exchange of currency within a year-and-a-half time span—in July, 1940; July, 1941; October, 1941. As a result, a man who had 1,000,000 Leis on July 1, 1940—a fortune at that time—would receive for them 40,000 rubles from the Russians who had taken over. On July 1, 1941 after the Rumanians re-occupied this area, that amount would be exchanged for 25,000 Leis. In October, 1941, this amount was exchanged for 600 rubles, for which the deportee later received 10 German Marks—the price of one loaf of bread!

Administrative Measures

Here is a decree containing regulations for the evacuation of Jews from several towns in Bukovina. The rules outlined are typical of the inhuman methods used everywhere in implementing the deportations.

Owing to the haste with which the measures were enforced, the decree appeared without number and date.

Measures with respect to the evacuation of the Jews from the city of Suceava, from the towns of Itkan and Burdujeni.

1. The city and the towns must be surrounded by guards and troops on the evening preceding (the evacuation).

2. On Oct. 9, 1941 at 7 A.M. the Prefect, the Mayors

of the municipalities, the Commander of the Gendarme Legion, the Commander of the Garrison, the Chief of Police and the representatives of the Jewish communities will be convened at the Prefect's Office and informed of the evacuation of (the Jewries of) these municipalities.

3. These measures will be announced by drum-beating and the reading of the pertinent decree to the Jewish population.

4. The departure will take place on Oct. 9, at 3 P.M. from Suceava.

5. The departure on Oct. 10 takes place at 1 P.M.

6. In order to take over the goods left by the Jews, committees of three or four will be set up.

7. A committee composed of the Prefect, the Director (of the local branch) of the National Bank and the Mayor will take over the jewels of the evacuated Jews.

THE DEPORTATIONS BEGIN

The stage being set, the deportations were carried out efficiently and cruelly. One could expect no more barbarism even from Dictator Antonescu, whom Hitler himself praised as "proceeding in these matters in a far more radical fashion than we have done up to the present."[29]

Timetable

Oct. 4—The Army Headquarters sends the deportation order to the Bukovina Military Command.

Oct. 5—Decree by the Military Cabinet ordering the "exchange" of the valuables and currency of the deportees.

Oct. 6—Ion Antonescu announces his decision concerning the new deportations to the Cabinet.

South Bukovina

On Oct. 4, the evacuation of Suceava, Compulung, and Radauti Departments began.

Dr. Mayer Teich, an outstanding Jewish leader and president of the Suceava Jewish community comprising 3,570 persons, gave a vivid account of the events in his town:

Already as early as August and September, the terrorism and vexations at the hand of the authorities became intolerable. We felt that some grave measure was being prepared. To my question Prefect Bratan answered that the establishment of a ghetto was envisaged. Some weeks later Col. Stroiescu took Col. Bratan's place. He, although a strict man, at the beginning was correct and attempted to ease the situation. But the terrorism was continued by Col. Zamfirescu, commander of the draft board, who without any official authorization interfered with everything. He threatened me, too, several times, "to put to the wall" for no reason whatever. The prefect told me on numerous occasions that Col. Zamfirescu should be interned into an asylum.

On Thursday, Oct. 9, 1941, at 5 A.M. a messenger from the Prefect's Office awoke me and called me to the office of the Deputy Prefect. On the street I found a number of Jews weeping; they heard that the Suceava Jews would be deported on the same day. I did not believe it and asked them not to create a panic. At 6 A.M. I entered the Deputy Prefect's office. There I found Maj. Botoreagu and the mayors of Suceava, Itkan and Burdujeni. The deputy Prefect opened an envelope pretending to have received it at that moment. He read the decree pertaining to the evacuation issued by the Army Headquarters. The decree imposed death penalty for disobedience, especially for failure to depart, failure to surrender the valuables, etc.

The decree contained the exact topography of the city so that I immediately saw that it was prepared here, in Suceava. It forbade us to take along anything except for hand baggage and food for eight days. When I asked why had such measures, equal to a death sentence, been taken against us, Maj. Botoreagu said:

"The higher interests of the State." It is interesting to
note that although to accept Jewish valuables for safekeeping was forbidden under the penalty of death, the
Deputy Prefect Ioachinescu, Major Botoreagu, and
Police Chief Apreutesii and other officials did accept
a large number of jewels from the Jews for safekeeping,
hoping that the owners would never return.

I departed with the third group . . . When the train
was ready to move, Col. Zamfirescu came and halted it
. . . he had given orders for the evacuation of those who
could not move. Soon aged and sick persons were
brought by carriages, wrapped in sheets without any
luggage. What's more, Dr. Bona, the chief physician of
the hospital, hustled out all Jewish patients, even
those whose condition was very serious, like Isaac
Mayer, a driver, one of whose feet was amputated a few
days before and who was in a coma. He died an hour
before our departure. Dr. Bona put out of the hospital
even his colleague, Dr. B. Wagner, a man over 70 in
grave condition. Unable to endure the pains, he killed
himself after our arrival in Moghilev. But the climax
was reached when they sent several patients suffering
from typhus abdominalis . . . Finally they brought a
number of insane . . . Zamfirescu shouted that he would
not leave one Jew here—the sick, the insane or those
suffering from contagious disease were all the same to
him. And all this without any authority. He shouted,
he howled, and terrorized everybody. There were horrible scenes, the insane howled, the sick wept, their families did not know what to do with them. Beside the
dead body of Isaac Mayer stood his little daughter with
a candle in her hand . . .

On Oct. 9 Dr. Filderman, on behalf of the Federation
of Jewish Communities addressed an appeal to Ion Antonescu.

On Oct. 10, the deportees arrived in Attachi, at the
Dniester, the gate of Transnistria.

New groups were deported from the three South Bukovina departments. From the town of Dorna Vatra and surrounding villages 2,650 Jews were dispatched within five hours.

Operation deportation continued with unabated fury. On Oct. 11 the last group of the Suceava Jews, together with the sick and insane, were deported. On that same day, Dr. Filderman made an appeal on behalf of the Kishinev Jews.

The evacuation of the three departments was completed by Oct. 13. Within five days 26,000 Jews had been deported. Only 182 Jews remained in South Bukovina: 79 in Campulung, 72 in Radauti and 31 in Suceava. They were spared because their services were indispensable. Most of them were professionals or specialists in lumber production. Dr. Schurtzer, for example, was the only gynecologist in Radauti. At the request of the authorities he was sent back from Attachi. Dr. Teitelbaum was the only dentist in the same city. All these experts remained in their homes until the end.

Czernowitz

At 7 P.M. on Oct. 9 the city was surrounded with a military cordon. No one could enter or leave. Two infantry regiments arrived to assist the police and gendarmerie.

Placards posted two days later announced the establishment of a ghetto. The Jews were "invited"—under death penalty—to move within eight hours into the ghetto.

Here is the "program" of this fateful day as fixed and publicized by the Governor, General Calotescu:

Program
of the
Concentration into the Ghetto of the Jews of Czernowitz
Oct. 11, 1941

7 A.M.   The assembling of the (leaders) of the Jewish
community of Czernowitz and its suburbs in the
Military Headquarters. The enclosed information,
Decree No. 38, and the regulations concerning the
Ghetto shall be read to them. It shall be announced
that all authorizations for public work are cancel-
led, thus the entire Jewish population has to enter
the ghetto.

8—9:30 A.M.   The leaders of the Jewish community
shall announce (the measures) to all Jews of Czernowitz. Simultaneously the organs of the Czernowitz Police will inform the Jewish population by
reading the decree at the intersections.

9:30 A.M.—6 P.M.   The interval accorded for the removal to the ghetto. The closing of the ghetto. No
one can enter the ghetto without a permit issued
by me.

The Governor of Bukovina
Gen. Corneliu Calotescu

In order to enforce this "program" Calotescu issued a
spate of draconic orders. Jews were permitted to take
along clothing and food. They were required to submit
to the authorities a list of their remaining property as
well as the keys to their houses. Their possessions passed
into the property of the State. (Decree No. 57-941)

The death penalty was imposed for:

1. Being found outside the ghetto after 6 P.M. of
Oct. 11.

2. Failure to obey orders.

3. Instigating others to disobey.

4. Selling gold or valuables to Christians.

In an act of unparalleled brutality, 50,000 people were
driven from their homes within eight hours.

In his "Confessions," Traian Popovici, the then Mayor
of the City, gives a dramatic account of the proceedings
in Czernowitz:

. . . After Gen. Calotescu took office the Jewish problem became the chief interest of his Military Cabinet. A veritable cascade of oppressive measures was issued: prohibition to exercise their professions; Jewish doctors were allowed to treat Jewish patients only; exclusion of the Jewish children from schools maintained by the state or the municipalities; prohibition to establish Jewish private schools; closing of the synagogues; prohibition to hold Jewish services; freezing of debts owed to Jews; obligation to do work "for the common weal," i.e., street-sweeping, repair of buildings, barracks, etc. without pay, and many other measures of oppression.

. . . A psychosis of madness seized the minds of many in leading positions distorting their mentality and making them accomplices of the disgrace which has been written by some amoral elements into the history of our nation.

. . . On Oct. 9, news reached Czernowitz to the effect that the Jews concentrated in the lagers of Storojinetz, Visnita, Vascauti and Lujeni had been entrained and sent forward to the Dniester . . . On the same day I was called to the Gubernatorial Office . . . here I learned that the mass deportation of the Czernowitz Jews had been decided. I was petrified. But I was able to blurt to the Governor: "Have you come to this pass, Mr. Governor?" He answered: "What can I do? This is an order of the Marshal and here are the delegates of the chiefs of the Army!" There were present Gen. Topor and a Lt. Col. Petrescu.

. . . At the City Hall my office was filled with the leaders of the Czernowitz Jews who, torn by care, were awaiting word of redemption. The city was seething with excitement. News of arrival of two gendarme battalions and of the impending ordeal spread like wildfire. I could not offer them any encouragement. I was speechless before their agitation, their instinct told them everything.

The morning of Oct. 11 was as cold and sad as the hearts of the many unfortunates. I looked out the window of my bedroom and amidst the flying flakes of the early snow I saw a scene which was incredible. In the streets was a vast crowd of wandering people. The aged were helped by children, there were women with infants in their arms, cripples dragging their lame frames. All had bundles in their hands or were pushing small carriages loaded with boxes. Some carried their burden on their backs: luggage, bundles of linen, cushions, blankets, clothing, rags. They were beginning their mute pilgrimage to their vale of tears, the Ghetto.

Only one who knows the topography of Czernowitz can grasp how inadequate was the space reserved for the Ghetto . . . This section that could hardly have accommodated 10,000 people had to house 50,000 Jews plus the Christian population which lived there . . . Many were forced to live in corridors, cellars, garages, under bridges, anywhere to find shelter against snow and rain. Of the hygienic conditions I don't even speak. No sanitary water to drink . . . the pungent smell of sweat, urine, and excrement, of loathsome humidity . . . exactly like the smell of a flock of sheep in the field.

I don't know whether it was so designed, but the effect was conspicuous: the exploitation, official and private, of these outcasts. Branches of the National Bank were opened in order to exchange foreign currency in ruble and to take over the jewels . . .

But let us turn to the non-official strategy which was tacitly permitted during the whole course of the deportations . . . Although the regulations strictly prohibited entry into the Ghetto, no one paid attention to them. On the second day (after its establishment) a whole caravan made for the Ghetto, women of all strata of society, well known go-betweens . . . hyenas who smelled carcasses. With assurances that they were on good terms with the Governor or Military Commander or someone else, the wholesale looting started. All that they, the victims, still had on them, gold coins, jewels, rugs, cloth or coffee, tea (was handed over) in the hope of obtaining exemption from the evacuation. Influence peddling was in full swing.

On Oct. 15, Marshal Antonescu in a telephone conversation with the Governor permitted the exemption from deportation of 20,000 Jews. That same afternoon . . . General Calotescu told us: "Gentlemen, the Marshal permitted the stay of 20,000 Jews. I cannot do the selection, I do not know the persons and the necessities. I authorize you, General (Ionescu) and you, Mr. Mayor, as well as you, Mr. Consul (Shellborn, German Consul) to make the selection. You know the men— and you, Mr. Consul, know the Reich's interest in the economy of this province.[30] The Consul asked to be excused, saying he could not act in an internal act of the country.

Now a new phase of activity started, the selection (of those to be exempted). First of all we decided to call upon the leaders of the Jewish congregation to prepare the lists as fast as possible . . . They needed two days for this work. They submitted 179 lists to us to which they added some more.

I succeeded in protracting the work until Nov. 15 when the Marshal ordered that all those who had not been deported shall remain. Those who remained here on the basis of Mayor Popovici's authorization (not signed by Governor Calotescu) were called 'Popovici's Jews' in contradistinction to the rest who were called 'Calotescu's Jews.'[31]

The deportation of the first group of the 30,000 non-exempted Czernowitz Jews began on October 13. In a surprise move some of the streets in the Ghetto were sealed off by a military cordon. The Jews in these streets were brutally forced to march to the depot and were shipped off.[32]

Oct. 14, the day that Ion Antonescu exempted 20,000 Czernowitz Jews from deportation, saw the budding of a shameless racket: exemptions were sold for "hard currency" (dollars, British pounds and gold coins). Those exempted were permitted to return to their homes, which in the meantime had been looted.

From Oct. 15-Nov. 15, thousands of "unauthorized Jews" were shipped to Transnistria. During this period 16,500 were definitely freed from deportation by Col. Calotescu, the governor. Four thousand Jews were freed by the Mayor. Seven months later the latter were deported.

The Villages Around Czernowitz

Some 8,000 Jews were brought to Czernowitz from such villages of Costesti, Broscauti, and Iodova Nova. On Oct. 22 they were transported to Marculesti, robbed again and again until they had nothing but the clothing on their body. At Jampol they were driven through a narrow bridge into Transnistria. Whoever fell into the Dniester was drowned. Nothing was done for his rescue.

Storojinetz, Dorohoi Department, and Kishinev

The 2,000 Jews who had been interned in the Storojinetz ghetto since the summer were deported on Oct. 13.

Doroboi Department had not been an organic part of Bukovina until 1938 when it was incorporated as the result of an administrative whim. For a month nothing happened there and it was hoped that deportation orders would not be extended to include this district. But on Nov. 5 the axe fell with the announcement of the impending deportation of the Jews. The evacuation began on Nov. 7 after the Jews had been thoroughly searched for valuables and robbed by the officials in charge.

The deportation of the Kishinev Jews to Transnistria began on Oct. 8. Five days later Mihai Antonescu, the Vice Premier, suspended it. The authorities ignored his decree and continued the evacuations—an eloquent sign of the chaos, confusion and lack of discipline in Fascist Rumania.

The horrors of this operation are dramatically presented in this appeal by Dr. Filderman to Ion Antonescu:

Oct. 11, 1941

Monsieur Marshal:

Today I received a desperate appeal from the leaders of the Kishinev ghetto. On the eighth of this month 1,500 persons left, most of them afoot, taking along only what they could carry in their hands, consequently all doomed to perish.

In the horrible cold many of them are naked, without food and without a possibility to buy food on a journey which is to last eight days in rain, cold and snow.

Only the sick, the aged and the children were taken by carriages.

But (in many cases) the sick were not spared either; also the women have to walk.

This is *death, death, death,* without any other guilt than to be Jews!

I implore you, Monsieur Marshal, do not permit such a crushing tragedy to happen.

Sincerely yours,
Dr. William Filderman
President
The Federation of the Jewish
Congregations in Rumania.

But the Marshal *did* permit it. Instead of remedying the situation, he published in every newspaper a poisonous reply heaping charges and slander on the Jews. The deportations continued until the entire ghetto was emptied.

The sufferings of the victims were terrible. Many went insane, others committed suicide, most of them clung tenaciously to their lives hoping against hope.

At the end of October, the last groups of the Kishinev

Jews were deported except for about 200 renegades.[33]

By December, the deportations were completed. Bukovina was Jewless except for the 20,000 Jews in Czernowitz and a small number of experts elsewhere.

Ion Antonescu true to his "ivory tower" policy now appeared on the scene and *post facto* delegated a "Commission of Inquiry" into the irregularities that took place in the course of the deportations. The Commission submitted its report on Dec. 31.[34] Its findings include certain "irregularities" of mass murders, concerning whose punishment, however, nothing further was ever heard.

The Distribution of the Loot

The confiscated valuables of the Jews were temporarily stored in the coffers of the National Bank of Rumania. Various government agencies competed for their possession. The Governor of Bukovina claimed all objects of non-precious metal. He took the household utensils for use in the military mess rooms. The National Bank took all objects of gold. The mint was awarded the coins of other metal. The jewels and objects of art were sold at public auction.

Epilogue

To recapture the psychopathic hate-filled atmosphere of these days, we insert here Ion Antonescu's answer to Dr. Filderman's dramatic letters. Here are its highlights:

> Twice you wrote to me about the shattering tragedy (of the Jews) and implore me in impressive words reminding me of my "conscience" and "humaneness" and emphasizing that you are obliged to appeal to me and "to me alone" on behalf of the Jews who are being transferred into the ghettos prepared for them beyond the Bug.
>
> In order to touch upon a tragic note you emphasize

that this measure is "death, death, death" without any other guilt than to have been born as a Jew.

Mr. Filderman, no one is more sensitive than I toward the sufferings of the humble and unprotected. I understand your grief, but you, all of you . . . should have understood my grief, which was the grief of an entire people.

Do you think, *did* you think of what was going on in our soul during the last year when Bessarbia was evacuated[35] and what is going on today when day by day, hour by hour, we pay with . . . blood, very much blood for the hatred with which your brethren of faith in Bessarabia treated us during our retreat, how they received us and how they treated us from the Dniester to Odessa and in the regions of the Sea of Azof?

But true to a tradition, you try to become an accuser instead of a defendant, pretending that you forget the matters which brought about the situation which you deplore. Permit me to ask you, and, through you, all the coreligionists whose applause grew louder as the blows dealt to us grew in severity. What did you do last year upon learning of the behaviour of the Bessarabia and Bukovina Jews toward the retreating Rumanian troops who until that time protected the fortune and peace of these Jews?

Let me remind you: . . . (Here he enumerates ugly atrocities committed, allegedly, by Jews against the retreating Rumanians.)

These criminals received the arriving Russians with flowers and celebrated them with exuberant joy. We have photographs to prove this.

During the Bolshevik occupation, those whom you now bewail, informed on good Rumanians, thus surrendering them to the orgies of the Russians and bringing grief and mourning into numerous Rumanian homes.

From cellars in Kishinev day by day horribly mutilated corpses of our martyrs are brought to light—thus were they rewarded for having stretched out a friendly hand to these thankless beasts.

These are acts of hatred bordering on madness which your Jews nurtured against our tolerant and hospitable people which today is dignified and conscious of its rights.

(There follow more loathsome atrocities laid to the unfortunate Jewish population of these provinces and then with a queer twist he finishes.)

I ask you why so much hatred on the part of some Russian Jews with whom we have never had any conflict?

But this hatred is a hatred against everyone, you included.

Do not sympathize, if you really have a soul, with those who do not deserve it; sympathize with those who do deserve it!

Weep with the mothers who lost their children amidst such tortures and not for those who dealt to us and to you so much evil.

Marshal Antonescu
Oct. 19, 1941

This, then, was Antonescu's answer—the cheapest, lowest type of demagoguery.

If any atrocities had been perpetrated against the retreating Rumanian troops, they had not been committed by 300,000 Jews. If atrocities had been committed by Jews, only those guilty were responsible for them, not all the 300,000 Jews—and surely not the babies.

Antonescu never did produce the "proofs" and "photographs" referred to in the letter, not even at his trial when questioned about the deportations. Nor did he mention at his trial those hair-raising atrocities enumerated in [but here left out of] his letter, although he certainly should have done so in order to justify his behavior. They were nonexistent and no one knew it better than he. Yet he resorted to the most outrageous demagoguery and readily sacrificed hundreds of thousands of innocents as a means of diversion in his predicament.

It was during the time of the deportations that the explosion of a time bomb destroyed the headquarters of the occupying Rumanian forces in Odessa killing General Glogojeanu and a number of officers and men. It was generally assumed that Jews were responsible. The press was forbidden to report on this event, yet the news of it spread rapidly, arousing intense indignation. Antonescu's letter, published on Oct. 27, capitalized on the national climate of hatred by inaugurating an organized campaign of slander and incitement. The anti-Semitic psychosis reached its climax during these days.

One of its consequences was that the Chamber of Lawyers called upon its Dean to disbar Dr. Filderman because, having intervened on behalf of the deportees, "he identified himself with the enemies of the country;" furthermore, all Jewish lawyers were to be disbarred for "having failed to protest against Dr. Filderman's action." This mass disbarment was never carried through but the fact that such a move was even contemplated reflects the mood of ugly irrationality in Rumania.

The Third Phase

1942—A BLACK YEAR

Jan. 20, 1942, is one of the blackest if not *the* blackest day in Jewish history—the date of the Wannsee Conference.

Reinhard Heydrich, the bloodthirsty head of the Sicherheitsdienst and "Protector of Bohemia and Moravia," had originally called this meeting for Dec. 8, 1941.[36] But it had to be postponed because one of those invited, S. S.

Maj. Lange, was busy that day having the deported Berlin Jews slaughtered near Riga.[37]

Despite the 20 years of propaganda and nine years of government, the Nazis had failed to fix clear cut methods and a final objective concerning the treatment of the Jews. That the Jews must be trampled underfoot and dealt with like sub-humans was clear and this was being done by evacuations, ghettos, despoliations, boycotts, pogroms, and sporadic massacres.

But now these henchmen who had become the masters of Germany wanted unified, concerted action. Hjalmar Schacht's pre-planned systematic emigration project had been shelved, when he fell from Hitler's grace (Jan. 6, 1939.[38] Alfred Rosenberg's "reserve" plan was never taken seriously.[39] And the unrealistic Madagascar project, calling for the colonization of the Jews in Africa, had also been scrapped.[40]

In order to "settle finally this problem," Reinhard Heydrich, acting under a brief of Goering, issued another invitation to a conference to be held on Jan. 20, 1942, in Berlin, Germany.[41]

In just a few hours the sixteen hangmen—the representatives of the S. S., the police, the ministries concerned —decided that:[42]

1. the Jews from Germany and the occupied territories shall be deported to the East;
2. those unfit to work "shall be dealt with specifically" (killed) ;
3. the able-bodied shall work under conditions to which they will succumb;
4. those who survive these murderous conditions shall be treated specifically. (killed) .

These horrifying decisions wrote the darkest chapters in the history of the Jews and of humankind in general.

Now, with most of Europe conquered and two-thirds of world Jewry trapped, Germany looked toward "the potentialities in the East."[43] There, in the shadow of the Eastern war zones, was to be the slaughter-house of eight million Jews. That they must all be destroyed had been the "Fuehrer's Order,"[44] and the pagan leaders and generals[45] of the Reich translated it into reality with Germanic thoroughness and Teutonic savagery.

The diplomatic machinery exerted extreme pressure on the governments of the subjugated countries to cooperate. The Quislings assisted willingly. Beginning on Apr. 28, 1942, train after train bound for Auschwitz left France from Drancy and the Vélodrome d'Hiver in Paris, and later from Vichy-France.[46]

In the Netherlands, Westerbork—"Holland's Drancy"— became the camp of concentration, from whence 5,742 victims left in July, 1942, for the gas chambers. They were to be followed by more than 100,000 of their brothers.[47] In Belgium, Malines was the clearing station. The first transport from it left for Auschwitz on August 4, 1942.[48] In Norway the Jews were concentrated in Berg, near Tonsberg. On Nov. 26, 1942, the first group of 532 was sent to Auschwitz.[49] And in Greece the deportation started on Mar. 15, 1943 from Salonika.[50]

Under such auspices the dark year of 1942 dawned upon European Jewry. In this atmosphere it had become the official policy in all of Nazi-Europe—with the glorious exceptions of Denmark, Finland, Bulgaria and the Italian Army and People[51]—that a segment of each country's population, a large number of its innocent citizens, were to be murdered in the name of Germany's psychosis.

Because of Ion Antonescu's close connections with the Germans, dating back to his prison days, there is good reason to believe that he was kept informed of the Nazi's

Jewish policies. At any rate, he and his henchmen were among the first to carry out these grim projects.

THE LAST DEPORTATIONS

In April and May Jewish leaders discovered that new deportations from Bukovina were imminent. All their efforts to avert them failed. "Beguiled into a state of haughty beatitude through their deceptive military successes, the Rumanian leaders remained deaf to the pleas of the Jews.[52]

The first deportees were those who seven months before had received exemptions from Czernowitz's Mayor, Traian Popovici, without due confirmation by the governor. By the end of the spring of 1942 Popovici was dismissed; his fall was to prove fatal for the 4,000 holders of his exemptions.

Their deportation started on Sunday, June 7. Maj. Stere Marinescu, the governor's right-hand man, was in charge. Although accepting a monthly bribe of 500,000 Leis (about $1,500-$2,000) from the Jews, he treated them with unmitigated ferocity and enforced their deportations with inhuman brutality. On June 7 he assembled his men at midnight and told them: "This is the time! Go to their homes, get them up quick and take them to the Maccabee" (sports-ground, a camp for concentration). The order was carried out. Horrible scenes followed. The victims knew what to expect . . . some put an end to their lives.[53]

One thousand persons were herded to the Maccabee. On Sunday they were subjected to corporal examination for valuables; the next day, June 8, they were shipped in cattle cars to Serebria, near Moghilev. Sixty insane, together with their physicians, were among them.

On the following Sunday, June 14, another group of a thousand was deported by similar methods. Among them were inmates of old-age homes, patients from the hospitals carried on stretchers in night gowns. A number of those possessing "Calotescu exemptions" were "illegally" included.

Two weeks later, another black Sunday brought 2,000 more victims. Again, some holders of Calotescu exemptions were seized; some were released after protest, others were not. Several of those released were apprehended a second time and deported.

These 4,000 were not the only victims. In the city of Dorohoi 450 Jews still remained. Months before, while they were working out of town, their families had been deported. Ever since they had been hiding out in the city. Now Governor Calotescu ordered them tracked down and deported. In Transnistria at the town of Serebria they rejoined their families and were driven together with them toward the Bug.[54]

By now deportation became the favored punishment of the Rumanian authorities.[55] It became a Damocles sword over the head of the Jewish population. Decree No. 55,500—June 27, 1942—"obligated every Jew to work for the common weal." Even a minor infraction of this obligation was punishable by deportation. To escape this dread penalty the Jews would offer any kind of bribe. Thus the administration of forced labor resulted in a source of large income for both civilian and military authorities. Ion Antonescu eventually delegated the administration of forced labor exclusively to the military authorities.[56] This military agency was headed briefly by Gen. Constantin Cepleanu, a man of sadistic proclivities. A number of his subalterns committed suicide because of the humiliations to which he had subjected them. During the 40 days of his administration he sent hundreds of Jews to Transnistria.[57]

In the middle of 1942 the Germans pressed for new deportations. They began a massive newspaper campaign. The semi-official "Bukarester Tageblatt" in Bucharest and "Donauzeitung" in Belgrade simultaneously carried alleged reports of a decision by the Rumanian government to deport within a year its entire Jewish population. Two days later the "Voelkischer Beobachter" in Berlin republished these reports.

The German diplomats in Bucharest urged the Antonescus for action. On Aug. 18 Martin Luther, the head of "Deutschland" Department of the Berlin Foreign Office, reported to Ribbentrop "that Mihai Antonescu's agreement with the Marshal is on record. According to it German agencies are at once to deport Jews from Arad, Timisoara and Turda."[58]

The German agencies made preparations. On Aug. 13, the Security Service, and on Sept. 26-28 the German Railroad Administration held conferences and resolved that the Rumanian Jews shall be concentrated in Adjud and transported to the death chambers of Belzec, Poland.

These were critical days for the Rumanian Jews. One frightening rumor followed another. No one dared to believe or disbelieve them. Finally from the office of the Administration of Jewish Affairs of Radu Lecca came the announcement that the government had decided to deport the Transylvanian Jews.

The Jewish leaders started a desperate fight to rescue their people. There are various versions of what happened.

It is certain that the leaders of the Transylvanian Jews—Dr. S. Ligeti, Dr. I. Tenner, both of Timisoara; Aladar Lakatos of Arad; A. Felter of Sibiu—hastened to Bucharest to ward off the danger.

The first to show any understanding was a Dr. Stroescu,

the personal physician of Ion Antonescu. He intervened with the dictator on behalf of the Jews after receiving 100,000,000 Leis (about $250,000) for the benefit of a hospital he had founded.

Queen Elena and the young king, Mihai I, warmly supported the rescue action. So did the Mitropolit of Transylvania, Balan. According to one source he made a special journey to Bucharest in order to intervene.[59] But according to the then Chief Rabbi Alexander Shafran, the Metropolit happened to be in Bucharest and when Shafran pleaded for his help, "the Mitropolit showed the correct frigid attitude in front of a Rabbi, but nonetheless he approached Ion Antonescu."

Also Monsignor Andrea Cassuto, the Apostolic Nuncio and René de Weck, the Swiss Ambassador, interceded with the dictator.[60]

Which of these actions was the decisive one, remains the secret of an accursed grave (that of Ion Antonescu). Nevertheless, as a result of some or all of them, the Jewish leaders were notified, without benefit of any official document, that the idea of deportation was dropped.

The mercurial and irresponsible Antonescu, a few weeks later (Oct. 10) was to order his Minister of Internal Affairs to deport the Jews of Transylvania. The categoric order contained elaborate instructions. Fortunately Gen. Picky Vasiliu disclosed its contents to I. Antal, a leader of the Transylvanian Jews. However, Dr. Antal's pleas with the general failed to move him. Antal returned shortly with Dr. Filderman and after hours of pleading their cause they finally succeeded in swaying the general. Picky then prevailed upon the dictator to withdraw the order for good.

Yet the deportation mania was still to claim 2,000 more victims.

On July 24, 1942, a decree ordered all Jews suspected

as communists to be deported to the horror camp of Vapniarka, Transnistria. As a result, at the beginning of September, 578 Jews were apprehended on the grounds that
a year before, during the Russian occupation of Bessarabia, they had applied for repatriation to that province.
Simultaneously in various towns and cities 554 communist
suspects were seized and were transported to Vapniarka
along with 407 Jewish communists who had been interned at Targu-Jiu. Their fate was shared by 148 Jews
and their families who were accused of infractions of the
forced labor laws.

These were the last groups of deportees. And by this
time, a note of hope was sounded. On Sept. 13, 1942, the
day of Rosh Hashono, U. S. Secretary of State Cordell
Hull in a special message warned the Fascists under
threats of heavy retaliations against continuing their atrocities. His threat had the effect of a bombshell. Even the
Bucharest daily, "Porunca Vremii," a paper which for
30 years had disseminated vicious anti-Semitic propaganda, changed its tone for one day. Instead of inciting
against the Jew it paid tribute to his heroism in enduring
his martyrdom in silence.

The change in the military situation was to bring an
improvement in the political climate, too, as we shall see
in a later chapter.

4

Transnistria:
The General Background

The Basic Decree

On Nov. 11, 1941, Gheorghe Alexianu, the governor of
Transnistria, issued Decree No. 23. Among its provisions
were the following:

1) The deportees shall dwell in houses forsaken by the
Russians or the native Jews.

2) A register of the Jews shall be set up in every settlement.

3) No Jew shall leave the town or city assigned to be
his place of dwelling.

4) Every settlement shall elect a leader for each group
of 20 and "a chief of the colony" shall be responsible for
the good order of things.

5) The Jews are obligated to perform work for the
common weal; the wages of unskilled laborers shall be one
Reichsmark, that of skilled laborers two RM a day.

6) Any Jew found outside the city or town of his residence shall be punished as a spy.

This decree became the constitution of the Transnistrian ghettos and camps. Its punitive measures were strictly and often inhumanly enforced.

The Epidemic

During the first winter (1941-2), a typhus epidemic raged throughout the Jewish camps in Transnistria. Its outbreak was inevitable.[1] The hygienic conditions were deplorable. The houses, mostly of clay, had no toilets, let alone bathrooms. The departees were forced to take care of their bodily needs in the yard. Aqueducts were unknown in these parts; they drew water from wells that were rank with filth. There were no public baths, no soap; the filth grew visibly on their bodies.

Anywhere from five to nine families were squeezed into places which normally sheltered one family. They slept on the floor, wrapped in the clothes they had worn during the day. Undernourished, they bartered clothing for food as long as they possessed any. The houses and their unfortunate inhabitants teemed with fleas and lice bearing infection. And the psychic shock inflicted by the deportee's sufferings further weakened their resistance.

As a result, soon after the arrival of the deportees in Transnistria, in November and December 1941, a typhus epidemic broke out and spread with unchecked rapidity. By January it had assumed disastrous proportions. Hundreds collapsed daily in the city of Moghilev, thousands in the countryside. The disease ravaged all Jewish camps and "colonies" throughout Transnistria.

Despite tremendous difficulties, the Jewish Committee in Moghilev established a pavilion in a ruined hospital and another one at a different location. Both were unheated but requests to purchase coal or wood were rejected by the authorities. There was neither kerosene nor soap for disinfection. A number of doctors and nurses soon contracted the disease and many of them died.

Dreadful suffering took place in the Moghilev hospitals.

The feet of some patients froze. There were no beds for the new patients who were brought in daily from the city and nearby towns. Half-frozen patients were laid down in the corridors and left there. The doctors' pleas to send them elsewhere were ignored.

The death toll was heavy. In Moghilev 7,000 contracted typhus, nearly 2,000 died. In nearby Shargorod of the 2,414 cases 1,449 (more than half) were fatal. Of the 27 attending physicians, 12 died.[2]

Farther east in the camps on the Bug's bank the devastation was even worse. In the city of Bershad and in the neighboring villages, no medical measures were taken at all. The number of the victims was 20,000. In the town of Ushtea 1,600 of 2,500 deportees died.

The dead were collected in carriages and thrown into mass graves. Often they were left in the fields. Official reports of Rumanian authorities admitted that about the half of the deportees were swallowed up by this epidemic.[3]

The hostile attitude of the Rumanian administration was responsible for the epidemic's unparalleled toll, as developments in the city of Moghilev so tellingly proved. The moment a decent man, Dr. C. Chirila, was appointed chief-physician of the Department, the situation began to improve. He took energetic measures concerning the cleaning up of the houses, yards and wells. He procured kerosene to rid the population of parasites. He trebled the number of beds in the hospitals. The effect was immediate: the number of cases dramatically declined and soon the disease disappeared completely.

The Mental Sufferings

The Rumanian authorities minced no words concerning their intentions.

At a conference of the Jews of the Moghilev Department the representative of the authorities, I. Mumuianu, said: "The inscription on the entrances of the cemeteries could be: 'Give up all hope, ye who enter this place! You too . . . bury all hope for your return to your places.' "[4]

Another representative of the government addressed the following words to the physicians meeting in Moghilev: "We sent you here to die, but you are expected not to have contagious diseases."

Pronouncements like these created an atmosphere of such despondence that many of the exiles lost their will to live.

Beatings and Forced Labor

Beating of Jews was a routine procedure in the Transnistrian camps. Police, soldiers, state and county officials freely beat up, kicked or clubbed the Jews. Civilians, acting under no official sanction, would frequently assault the hapless prisoners.

In Moghilev whenever a Jew was summoned to the gendarmerie he was received with a hail of strokes regardless of his social status or of his guilt or innocence. In Bershad, one police officer, Lt. Grigorescu, practiced as a kind of sport the beating of the Jews for no reason. In Vindiceni a S. Rachlitzki indulged in the same pastime; although a manager of the sugar factory, he had no official standing at all.

Governor Alexianu's Decree No. 23 obligated the Jews to perform "work for the public good." In Moghilev the Jewish Committee succeeded in organizing forced labor in a human way. But in all other places especially in Peciora and Tulcin—as we shall see—labor was used in true Nazi fashion as a means of extermination. Both men and women, were driven like cattle irrespective of their training, education, fitness, and state of health. Ill-clad, some of them half-naked, they had to perform heavy physical work in the murderous Russian winter. In the evening they brought back those who had frozen to death. The authorities provided neither food nor tools and implements. The Jewish relief committee in Bucharest sent large quantities of shovels and tools to their enslaved brethren.

Nor were the authorities keen on paying the pittance of wages provided for in the decree. In Moghilev during the first eight months instead of the 160,903 RM due for the labor performed, 21,483 RM was paid; during the first year and a half the Jews received instead of 387,865 RM, the sum of 56,358 RM.[5]

Grueling work in inclement weather without adequate nourishment led to the same results here as in other parts of the Nazi world.

Ghettos and the Yellow Badge

During the first nine months the exiles were not segregated. They lived in ruined buildings wherever they found them. In June, 1942, however, ghettos were set up all over Transnistria. Moghilev's prefect, C. Nasturas, spearheaded the action. In his Decree No. 147, June, 1942, he ordered the establishment of a ghetto as "A matter of Rumanian honor and dignity."

By July 1 the Jews in the entire department were herded into ghettos. The 15,000 Jews in the City of Moghilev were squeezed into a few streets, 20-30 in a room. Many families slept in the open air. Such was the situation in all of the Jewish settlements.

Ever since their arrival in Transnistria the Jews had had

to wear an identifying yellow badge in the form of the star of David. They were ordered to wear it even within the confines of the ghetto. In the Shargorod and Smerinca ghettos all Jewish houses were marked with yellow stars.

Evacuations

Even as a beast cannot be restrained from lacerating its victim, so the Nazis could not be induced by any means to spare the Jews.

Engineer Jaegendorf's hope that the signal services rendered by the Jewish laborers and professionals would earn them the right of residence in Moghilev proved unfounded.

The Nazis in Poland and Russia exterminated hundreds of thousands of fine Jewish craftsmen and agriculturists,[6] sacrificing the higher interest of war production for the sake of their obsession. The Moghilev prefect, Col. Constantin Nasturas, followed their precedent. In his order of July 5, 1942, he decreed that the Jewish skilled laborers shall be removed from the factories. "At the time of the establishment of our industrial undertakings we needed the Jews; now there is no sense in keeping them any longer. We shall remain here with the Ukrainians but not with the Jews."

Such was the mentality of this man, a poet of national fame. While poets and scholars of other nations, as a rule, were champions of high ideals, many, if not most, of the Rumanian literary luminaries were of a different stripe. The greatest Rumanian poet, M. Eminescu, the brilliant Transylvanian poet, Octavian Goga, the foremost Rumanian scholar, Nicolae Jorga, were all consumed with anti-Semitism and prejudices of every description.

Col. Nasturas had begun his initiative against the Moghilev Jews in early 1942. On Feb. 16 he ordered the Jewish Committee to send experts to the town of Scazinetz with a view to preparing a plan for the evacuation of 4,000 Moghilev Jews to that town. The Jewish Committee, using delaying tactics, succeeded in stalling this move.

However, on May 19th Governor Alexianu decreed the following:

1) Four thousand of the Moghilev Jews must be selected for evacuation to Scazinetz.

2) Their number is to include 10 rabbis, 10 physicians, 10 midwives, 50 craftsmen.

3) In Scazinetz they shall engage in agriculture and shall receive land for that purpose in exchange for 600,000 Leis ($1,500).

4) They shall be supplied with food by the Moghilev Jews. The food shall be transported in carriages drawn by men.

5) The Moghilev Jewish Committee shall provide them with 200 shovels and 200 pushcarts.

The interventions and pleas of the Moghilev Jewish Committee were fruitless. From May 29, to June 3, 3,000 Jews were sent to Scazinetz. On June 28 a group of 500 followed them. Escorted and beaten by the gendarmes, they were marched to their destination. The promise of agricultural pursuits was not kept. Scazinetz, was to become the grave of most of the evacuees.

Having received authority from the governor (Decree No. 28937, July 3, 1942), Col. Nasturas on Oct. 12 ordered the evacuation of 3,000 Jews to the dreaded death camp of Peciora. Gen. Iliescu took what he thought a wise measure in ordering evacuation of the poorest since they were doomed to perish by hunger anyhow.

The panic-stricken victims began a frenzied search for hiding places. But the police, aided by bloodhounds, tracked them down in cellars, attics, cornfields, trenches—wherever they took refuge. They were transported by train to Peciora, 80 persons in each frieight car; many of them died on the way.[7]

For half a year there was a lull in evacuation activities. Then, in the early part of May, 1943, one thousand laborers were sent to another death camp at Trihatz, in Oceacov Department. The conditions there are described in a later chapter.

Toward the end of that month, Prof. Alexianu, the governor of Transnistria, received a report on the Danilov case. Two years earlier Danilov, (first name unmentioned), a Czernowitz lawyer, had bribed the then prefect with one million Lei for permission to reside in the city of Moghilev. Danilov was courtmartialled and acquitted. The irate governor now ordered that Danilov and the innocent Moghilev Jewish Committeee be sent to the penalty camp of Vapniarka. He also ordered that all Jews in that province be removed to camps on the Bug's bank. Had this decree been enforced it would have spelled death for most of the exiles.

At this critical moment William Filderman arrived in Moghilev, not as a visitor, but as a deportee. Ion Antonescu had personally issued the decree for his expulsion following Filderman's protest against the levy upon the Rumanian Jews of four billion Leis; he had scored it as an unbearable burden, an act of confiscation of all Jewish properties . Filderman spent two months (June-July 1943) in Moghilev. Although a member of the German Todt made an unsuccessful attempt on his life, Filderman, the most heroic figure of Jewry throughout Nazi-Europe, continued undaunted in his brave fight for his fellow Jews. He frequently intervened even in his exile on behalf of the Jews in Moghilev Department. Yet he was powerless to prevent new waves of evacuations.

From June 8 on vast and undetermined numbers of Moghilev and countryside Jews were sent to the neighboring department of Tulcin. There a vast turbine was constructed at the cost of untold numbers of Jewish lives. Details of their sad story will be related later.

Orphans

There were thousands of orphans in Transnistria. Among them were children whose parents were massacred in 1941 as well as "living orphans," who were the children of evacuated Jews. Before their departure from Moghilev to one of the death camps parents left their children behind to save them from the worst.

There was no one to look after them. In a situation where all are starving and parents are unable to nourish their own children, who could be expected to take care of strangers? Thus the orphans were neglected, hungry, hopeless charges.

Yet Jewish charity did its utmost to save them. Orphanages were established, three in Moghilev, one in Shargorod —the only such institutions set up by deported Jews in Nazi-Europe.

But the help offered was inadequate. On Nov. 28, 1942, the Moghilev Jewish Committee reported that there were 796 orphans in the three institutions; during winter the orphanages were unheated; because of the inhuman cold many children could not leave their beds even to go to the bathroom; the air in the rooms was intolerable; undernourished children suffered from scabs and various skin diseases; mortality was high, in some months 10% of the children died.[8]

Slowly, as relief from Bucharest reached the deportees, the conditions improved. Their nutrition was more adequate and from May, 1943 not a single death occurred.

5

Camps and Ghettos of Transnistria

Moghilev Department

This department was a large center of deportation. In the
fall of 1941 approximately 60,000 persons were sent here—
15,000 to the city of Moghilev, the rest to the surrounding
smaller towns and villages. Two years later, in September
1943, the official report of the Gendarmerie Inspectorate
established that 32,002 Jews remained in this area. Allowing for those who had been evacuated, this figure indicates
a 40% decrease in the number of the exiles. These perished
because of epidemics and privations.

"THE GATES OF ENTRY": ATTACHI, COSAUTZ, REZINA

There were three "gates of entry" into the inferno of
Transnistria. We know little about Cosautz and Rezina,
but the diary of Dr. Mayer Teich gives a faithful account
of what happened in Attachi. Conditions in the other two
places were undoubtedly no different.

On Oct. 13, 1941, early in the morning our train
stopped . . . outside the Attachi station . . . We had to
leave the coaches hurriedly. The attitude of the soldiers
who escorted us had shown from the beginning how
deeply we had sunk. In their eyes we were no longer
human beings but mangy dogs with whom any joke and

trick is permissible. The luggage had to be thrown into a roadside ditch and be covered with straw. Rain mixed with snow drenched us and caused us to tremble— a human herd surrounded by armed beasts.

The aged and the sick, too, had to stay in the rain. Round about lay corpses left by former groups of exiles. It occurred to none to bury them. Two of our old people writhe in coma. Probably we shall abandon them too . . . God who forsook us may grant them unconsciousness and a swift end.

What I feel deeper than the physical suffering and even than the worry for my loved ones is our terrible humiliation. Without any guilt, without any reason, a *capitis diminutio* (death-penalty).

In all eyes you can read this "Why?". The commiseration with your loved ones whom until now you could protect and whom now you impotently see exposed to the forces let loose by man or nature . . . causes you a pain so fierce that you would yell, you would beat, you would war with God.

Whence shall we draw enough energy to be able to improve somehow this desperate situation, to procure food, to negotiate with the peasants concerning the transportation of men and things . . .

After a few hours . . . we received orders to march ahead to the town. Carriage-owning peasants, the first hyenas, asked enormous amounts for carrying us to the town of Attachi . . . My protest to Captain Popescu was partly successful as he reduced the fare to 2,000 Leis, i.e., to only the twentyfold of the regular fare . . . Then Capt. Popescu "benevolently" warned us to get quickly through the formalities of the National Bank and of the Customhouse—he wanted to get rid as soon as possible of us.

Thus we marched on the slippery road in quagmire mixed with large pieces of rock—the aged and the invalids with some belongings on the carriages, the rest of us, walking on both sides. We had to be appreciative of this favor as we were reminded that the former groups were not permitted to hire carriages, their aged and sick were left behind, prey for the beasts, human and animal . . .

We arrived in Attachi, or more precisely in the place where it once existed. The lower part of the town was assigned to us, the former Jewish section on the bank of the Dniester. As a result of the bombardment all houses were burned down or ruined. Walls with holes in them, here and there a roof or a part of a roof, blood and mud, everywhere were traces of the pogrom that destroyed the entire Jewish population of this place. Corpses in the streets, yards, cellars—all over. On many a wall inscriptions: "You who will come here, say a Kadish for (a name) ." "We died for the *Kidush Hashem* (sanctification of God's name) !" or "Here was murdered (a name) with all his family." Few from Attachi escaped with their lives. A young girl from Attachi, whom two years later I placed in an orphanage, had no idea through what miracle she had been saved during the pogrom. At a festival she sang a beautiful song about the Attachi Jewish martyrs.

Here, among the ruins, we found thousands of dazed men looking for food. Nowhere was there an empty place. Capt. Popescu offered us the Great Synagague. But we found only a few walls without rooves within which men were crowded, looking with horror at us. They knew what the arrival of new exiles meant. They thought that because of us they would be driven across the Dniester, where they would be tortured and exposed to the entire gamut of sufferings worse than death. It was possible that at that moment some of them felt hostility against us. In the struggle for life, for a piece of bread or for a corner to rest, even in the gutter, man becomes an animal baring his teeth at whoever draws near and may dispute his possessions."

As a result of our coming some of the earlier deportees were driven ahead. I placed my belongings in a vacant chamber which to some extent was protected from the rain. Then each of us went to search for a shelter, for any small corner in which to spend the night; but few succeeded in finding one. Most of us remained under the open sky. The gravely sick and aged with no family were placed in a house which had no doors or windows, only a dry floor and a roof. After nightfall I visited my aunt, Golda Breiner, an 87-year-old woman who could hardly recognize me. Beside her on the floor lay her husband Shaye Langer, over 92, one of the most respected businessmen of Bukovina, who still prided himself on the fact that he was one of the delegates to the first Zionist Congress in Basel . . . His wife whispered to him that I was there and he asked me to step nearer. I knelt down beside him, he grasped my hand and held it clasped with trembling strain for a long time. For a while he couldn't talk, the tears stifling his voice; then he gathered himself and said:

"Dear Doctor, how is it possible that they drive me away from Suceava? I was born there ninety years ago. I lived and worked there. I took over my father's store and ran it for sixty years. I had been Imperial Councillor (under the Austrian regime), City Councillor, leader of the Congregation. I've never had any fight with anyone and was honored and liked by all. You must promise me that you'll send memoranda to all competent authorities explaining to them all I told you and ask them to send us back, me and my wife, as we are two old people. In Suceava we have already prepared the graves for both of us. They should permit us to die there . . ."

Tears gushed from his eyes, he couldn't continue. Nor could I suppress my tears. I promised everything in order to soothe him. Within an hour he expired. I buried him on the Dniester's bank . . . His wife endured all the sufferings of Transnistria and had the strength to return to her native city, where she died.

You who in these days were sheltered under your rooves and slept in your beds, will not be able to form even a slight idea of how much we suffered, how terrifying our pains were and how tragic it is to die far away from your home. *YIZKOR!* Remember those who died on the roadside.

The shadows of night descended on Attachi. Dusk, darkness, rain, dirt, shouts, crying. Still there are peo-

ple on their feet. Parents lost their children, children
their parents. Chaos! They search, they shout, they howl,
they whisper. Hunger, pains, despair, death. In vain is
any attempt at comfort or consolation. No food can be
found, they go to sleep hungry, aware of the horror of
the morrow that must come and wishing that the night
may be long and calm. Almost nobody sleeps. But the
night passes rapidly as we behold the daybreak with
trembling heart. Very early in the morning the peasants
came with some bread and milk. But the prices are
phantastic [sic], most of us were unable to pay it.

Suddenly from a distance muffled voices are heard.
They intensify more and more and are finally into yells:
"The Jews from Edineti have come! They're naked and
hungry driven by a pack of wolves."

They're here already! Never shall I forget this scene.
They are no longer human beings. Hungry, clad in rags,
they drag themselves, tremble, moan, yell. In the bottom
of their eyes is the fear of death even as in the eyes of
hunted animals fleeing before a pack of hounds amidst
whining bullets. This herd of men beaten with whips
and arms march with uniform, strained, almost uncon-
scious motions. The beasts do not permit any of them to
stop and drive them ahead in the direction of the
Dniester, the raft, the inferno. But we surround them
and in a split second of confusion we succeed in slipping
some food or clothing into their hands, even in steal-
ing some of them and hiding them in our ranks. However, the soldiers quickly break up our cordon and now
I hear for the first time: "Whoever lags behind will be
shot dead!" I was to hear this all too often.

I see clearly our whole future. I cast a glance at my
son who, just recovering from a grave illness, would
need rest and nourishment. My eyes meet the stunned
eyes of my wife whose only thought and worry is her
son. When my thoughts turn toward my aged mother
and all those dear to me a wild pain seizes me, a tremble,
a spasm and swoon. I hear my wife whisper: "Let's
swallow the poison which we took along with us at our
departure from Suceava." My boy opposes it. With the

thirst for life of his 18 years, he finds all sorts of arguments and objections against such a decision. I don't know which of his arguments is the most persuasive one. Perhaps that of vengeance.

In order to encourage us, he, still weak of body and immature of mind, takes the initiative in his hand. He makes friends with Dr. Abraham Reicher, a 33-year-old man, a tower of strength, and confers with his brother-in-law, Samuel Neuberger. They form the first cell of resistance . . .

. . . None of them was granted to taste the joy of victory. S. Neuberger died on Feb. 26, 1942. Dr. Reicher followed him on March 3. Both were victims of typhus. My son died on Aug. 15, 1943. Two days later I placed him in the same coffin with his mother, my saintly wife, Ana Teich, who could and would not survive her only child. (Probably committed suicide.)

YIZKOR! Think of the noble martyrs, the saints who were chosen from among the hundreds of thousands of victims to remain in the soil of Ukraine. Our dead could at least be cared for until the last moment. Their last glance met the love-filled eyes of their dear ones. They were brought to Kever Yisroel and memorial stones guard their graves. But think of those whose last look met the eyes of their enemies, who died alone, forsaken, by hunger, or drowning or by bullets without ever being buried. I saw their corpses at Scazinetz, Spicot, Peciora and Nemirov.

Attachi! Who could describe Thee? ! . . . Who would understand (your horrors) who did not see robust men suddenly dropping dead on the ground or sturdy persons unexpectedly losing their minds. I still see Mrs. Rose Stein, widow of Dr. Stein, the lawyer, who thought she was in her home town and was straying through unknown streets. How politely did the poor woman ask right and left: "Please, be good enough to lead me to my house. I live in the house in which the Weiner bookstore is located." I see those unfortunates who all of a sudden burst into shouts, demanding food or else they would take the first train and go home!

This was Attachi. Yet incredible as it may sound, this was not the worst aspect of this place. Dr. Teich and his group belonged to the contingent of Bukovina Jews which was brought by train, like princes, to Attachi. But the Bessarabian Jews and a large segment of the Bukovina Jews who had been deported three months before did not travel by train; they were marched on foot to the banks of the Dniester. For three months they languished in the infernos of the Secureni, Edineti, Vartujeni and Marculesti camps. Now these ghost-like human wrecks were driven through the gates of entry. Among them were the Edineti Jews described so dramatically in Dr. Teich's account.

Such was Attachi and such were Cosautz and Rezina, the other gates of entry.

The indignities inflicted on the Jews there were twofold:

1.) The deportees had to go through the "Custom House", i.e., a last-minute search and robbery by the authorities. Amazingly, many of the Jews succeeded in hiding and retaining considerable amounts of money.

2.) With the confiscation of their personal papers and documents, the Jews lost their identity. Henceforth they were official numbers, not human beings.

THE ATTACHI-MOGHILEV ROAD

From Attachi the road led across a bridge over the Dniester and ran straight to Moghilev, the capital city of the Department of Moghilev. The road was only a few miles long, but it was the scene of endless sufferings for the exiles.

The first groups came from the Secureni camp. Soon those from Edineti followed. During their stay in the camp they had become destitute, possessing only what covered their bodies—if their bodies were covered. In the early, severe Russian winter many of them were half-naked. Thus they were driven in the deep, clay-like mud of the Bessarabian roads exposed to the cruelty and "jokes" of their guards. One of the favorite jokes was to throw some of the Jews into the Dniester to see whether the miracle of the Red Sea would repeat itself.

Many succumbed to exhaustion or were killed. The corpses were not buried, they remained in the fields where dogs and crows finished the work of men. Occasionally a mother, undeterred by the threat of being shot, scooped with her fingers a hole in the frozen soil in which to hide her dead child.

They spent their nights in ruined buildings, in stables, pigsties, barns. The walls often bore the names of those martyrs who, utterly exhausted, despondently waited for the moment when death would release them from their sufferings. The term *Toitenwand* (Wall of Death) was coined in those days.

THE CITY OF MOGHILEV

Almost half of the deportees—55,913 in number—passed through the city of Moghilev.[1]

The city lay in ruins. At the beginning of the war it had been subjected to severe bombardment. Most of the houses had no doors or windows, many were roofless.

The first miserable deportees coming from the Edineti or Secureni camps and most of those hailing from Czernowitz and South Bukovina were sent into the villages of Moghilev Department. They had to march on roads transformed into a quagmire by autumnal rains. At the intersection of the Moghilev-Ozarinet roads, 28 people became hopelessly trapped in the mud. Their desperate scramble only caused them to sink still deeper in the mud. The gendarmes did not permit anyone to help them. When a lawyer, Dr. Abraham Shapiro of Suceava, protested he was shot dead. All 28 victims perished.[2]

For eight weeks (Sept. 16-Nov. 17) about 40,000 persons were transferred into 50-60 villages and towns in the vicinity of the city of Moghilev.[3] Some of the Czernowitz Jews, who succeeded in concealing money and valuables, hired vehicles to reach their destination. They entered into an agreement with the prefect and sub-prefect of the Department and paid 6,000,000 Leis (about $15,000) an exorbitant amount for this privilege.

Some groups took another line of action. For a consideration of 1,000,000 Lei ($2,500) two Jewish leaders, Danilov and I. Malcash, received licenses for 800 Jews to stay in the city of Moghilev. Other groups offered skilled labor with a view to repairing war damages, to restoring bombed out factories and public utilities. Some 5,000 Jews obtained official permission by these means to remain in Moghilev. Another 10,000, who stayed illegally, lived in constant fear of expulsion.

MOGHILEV JEWRY ORGANIZED

At the end of November, a week after the issuance of the Basic Decree, the Moghilev prefect appointed a Jewish Committee of fifteen members which was to elect its own officers. Since Jews were forbidden to enter the offices of any local authorities, they had to channel all their requests through this committee.

Engineer S. Jaegendorf, a man of dynamic personality, was elected President of the Committee whose members included Dr. Mayer Teich, the former head of the Suceava

Jewish community, now the leader of the Shargorod settlement; F. Laufer; H. Kastner; S. Schaeffer; E. Pressner; Moses Katz and others.

Efforts had been made to organize the shapeless masses of the deportees even before this date. In October, 1941, thousands upon thousands of deportees crossed the city of Moghilev. In view of the large number of the aged, of women and children, it would have been inhuman to let them march in the cold, rainy weather. An organization was therefore created by the Jews to provide their transportation with money raised by a system of taxation.

Another pre-committee organization was that headed by Jaegendorf at the Prefect's order. Jaegendorf organized into a colony the nearly 1,000 men working on his projects to restore an electric plant and a munitions factory. They set up a collective bakery, purchased food collectively, had their own medical service and even their own pharmacy.

Soon other groups were formed—one, comprising 1,400 men, for the reconstruction of outbombed buildings; Dr. Danilov's group of 800 men and others.

All of these groups, however, were fragmented. The program of the Jewish Committee was all-embracing. Among its objectives were:

To create order in the chaos of 15,000 Jews thrown together in the city and possibly among the 40,000 in the villages and towns of Moghilev department;

To render services to the municipality and the county in order to assure their right to stay in the city and their very survival;

To feed the impoverished who otherwise would die of hunger;

To care for the orphans and the sick;

To put an end to the wild man-hunts which took place whenever the authorities needed laborers.

The difficulties confronting the committee were enormous. It had no suitable premises for an office, no desks, not even a sheet of paper. It was besieged by a desperate mass of men and women clamoring for immediate help. Yet in time the committee succeeded in setting up a network of institutions that included:

—an Old Age Home with 250 beds for old people without families;

—two Jewish Hospitals; the lager hospital and Dr. Lehrer's Hospital;

—a Hospital for Contagious Diseases including three pavilions, each with 100 beds;

—Public Kitchens which daily dispensed food to some 5,000 people;

—on Orphanage accommodating 50 children;

—a Bureau of Public Work which provided the authorities with the number of men required for forced labor;

—a Bureau of Vital Statistics;

—a Post Office.

These offices were to become vital organs in the life of the hapless masses. The public kitchens offered a piece of bread and a plate of food to those who otherwise would have remained unfed. The institutions sheltering orphans and the solitary aged provided care for persons who had been left to their fate.

The Bureau of Vital Statistics issued documents restoring the identity of those exiles whose papers had been destroyed. It gave information to despondent relatives who besieged it with inquiries on the whereabouts of departed family members.

The Bureau of Public Work created order in the field of forced labor. Originally whenever the authorities needed men for work they dispatched gendarmes who brutally seized in the streets men and women—a number of whom were aged, sick or incapacitated. The labor bureau maintained registers of able-bodied workers and rotated the laborers it sent out. Their fine work in reconstructing the sugar factory, the electric plant and the arms factory was appreciated by all concerned.

Here, as in Poland, the Jews hoped that through hard and valuable work they might find mercy from their taskmasters.[4] And like their Polish brothers, they were to find their hopes shattered. Without funds, with steadily decreasing revenues derived from the taxation of the "better class" deportees, with only meagre aid from the non-deported Jews, these organizations were unable to cope fully with the awful realities—massive poverty, inhuman housing conditions, unabated hostility from the authorities, acts of violence by state officials and gendarmes.

Yet the work of the Committee will remain a chapter of immortal glory in the annals of Jewry, of heroic efforts to start a new life in a hostile, hate-blinded environment.

RURAL CAMPS AND GHETTOS

In September 1943 53 rural ghettos existed in Moghilev department; 24 of them included less than 100 deportees, 22 less than 500, while seven had more than 1,000 inmates. The largest of these ghettos were at Shargorod (2,971), Djurin (2,871) and Murafa (2.605), followed by Ciopaigorod (1,295), Lucinetz (1,107), Popiviti (829) and Balki (680).

Although life in the city of Moghilev was an inferno, it was regarded as Paradise by those in the rural ghettos. Here is a report made by Moses Katz, of the Moghilev Jewish Community, after his visit to these ghettos.[5]

. . . during my visit I discovered in the town of Co-notcauti, near Shargorod, a long and dark stable standing alone in a field. Seventy people were lying in it in a mess, men, women, children, half-naked and miserable. It was horrible to look at them. They all lived on begging. Their head was Mendel Aronevici, a former banker in Darabani, Dorohoi Dept. He too lived in abject misery.

In the ghetto of Halcintz they ate the carcass of a horse which had been buried two yards beneath the ground. The authorities poured acidum carbolicum on it, yet they continued eating it. I gave them some money, food, clothing and took their promise not to touch that carcass. I placed them in a nearby village and paid the rent for three months in advance. The Jews in Grabvitz lived in a cave. I had to remove them to the village against their will. They couldn't part from the seven hundred graves of their loved ones who had been buried near their cave.

I found the same scenes at Vinoi, Nemerci, Pasinca, Lucinetz, Lucincic, Ozarinetz, Vindiceni,—everywhere men exhausted, worn out; some of them worked on farms, others in the tobacco factory, but the majority lived on begging.

The relief from Bucharest was far too meager to cope with their mass of misery.

The chief of the lager in Promeshanita reported to the Jewish Central Office in Bucharest:

Within the last two years I received about 500 Rm for the 70 souls in my lager. The box of clothing you sent me contained a few pieces of women's apparel, a couple of high hats, two pyjamas, one tuxedo and a few pairs of gloves. Imagine—what a sight it would be if Hershel Cohn, who can't leave the lager for being entirely naked, appeared in Promeshanita wearing a tuxedo, top hat and gloves!

The stories of the individual camps are not known. We have some sketchy information about three camps only.

Shargorod

The camp originally accommodated 7,000 inmates.[6]
Their scourge was one Dindelegan, the pretor (first name
unmentioned). Although he was a lower administrative
official, the power over the Jews of any official was literally unlimited in those days of madness. According to Dr.
Teich, the leader of this ghetto, Dindelegan was a schizo-
phrenic. At times he was quite reasonable, at others he
behaved like a savage.

On Nov. 16, 1941, a group of Dorohoi Jews was marched
through Shargorod, their destination farther east. Their
misery shook even the Ukrainian population so deeply
that the peasant women who had brought food for sale
donated it to them instead. Then they begged Dindelegan
on their knees to permit this group to stay in the town.
The pretor granted the request—for a sizeable consideration.

During the first winter the typhus epidemic claimed an
appalling number of dead. Their burial was almost impossible. With the thermometer frequently dipping to
40° Celsius below zero, huge piles of wood had to be
burned in order to soften the ground enough for graves
to be dug. During the Shargorod epidemic, the physicians
worked heroically—12 of 27 died from typhus.[7] After the
death of Dr. Hermann and Dr. Harth their wives committed suicide.

These tragedies failed to prevent Dindelegan and a
colleague from Ciopaigorod from acts of shameless extortion. They charged 5,000 Leis per person for permission to stay. This they demanded in the middle of the
winter when they knew they had the Jews at their mercy;
to march to another lager in that weather would have
meant certain death. After haggling they accepted one-

and-a-half million Leis (about $3,750), instead of the originally demanded 25-30 million Leis.

Nothing throws sharper light on Dindelegan's savagery and the general lawlessness than the case of the six Jews who on Mar. 20, 1942 walked from Shargorod to Djurin. Leaving the ghetto was a crime punishable according to the military penal code (Decree No. 23 by the Governor). At the moment that they were seized by a policeman on the road, Dindelegan happened to be passing by in a truck. He took them to Shargorod and surrendered them to the police headquarters for immediate execution. Dr. Teich hurried to the pretor and pleaded with tears in his eyes for the life of the six innocents. Dindelegan answered that it was too late, the men were already in the hands of the police. Dr. Teich went next to police headquarters and then to the cemetery where they had been taken for execution. On his way he heard the blast of a volley. Upon his arrival at the cemetery he found the victims dead, surrounded by weeping Ukrainians.[8]

The number of orphans was very large in Shargorod as in most ghettos. An orphanage was established to which 152 orphans were admitted in June 1942. Within half a year these emaciated unfortunates were restored to health and normalcy. Amidst the ghastly events in this camp, the story of these rehabilitated orphans is the only ray of light.

Bar

Situated near the Russian border, Bar was the scene of a terrible slaughter. The boundary line was not respected by the German Einsatzgruppen "who with the connivance and active help of the *Reichswehr*"[9] destroyed within one year more than one million Jews in the Russian territory.[10] On Oct. 20, 1942 they penetrated into this Rumanian-occupied place and ordered all the Jews of that region assembled. The 12,000 persons who gathered were driven out of town and machine-gunned. Many a child was thrown alive into the mass grave that had been prepared in advance. Babies were seized by their feet and torn in two. Despite this *Gross-aktion* a year later (in January 1943) there remained some 1,200 Jews in this region. They were sent to a lager in the nearby village of Bolchis. There they were herded into a stable and forbidden to buy food. Five hundred of them perished of starvation. The fact that the official report of 1943 does not include Bolchis in the register of the ghettos indicates that the remaining 700 must have perished, too.

Scazinetz

Moses Katz, gives the following account of this "colony."

In Scazinetz, his report says, there were two rows of barracks—one for those of better circumstances, the other for the paupers. The barracks had no roofs, windows or doors. To cross the path that divided the two rows was punishable by death.

The inmates were starving. A few times weekly wild-pea soup was brought from Moghilev in carriages drawn by Jews. The inmates supplemented this fare with grass and leaves with which they tried to quell their nagging hunger. Mr. Katz saw Engineer Oxman of Czernowitz who subsisted on this diet; he was bloated by hunger like many others and died within a few days.

There was one well in the whole lager, its water full of mud and dirt. Mange, diarrhea, starvation decimated the Jews. In the fall of 1942 when the lager was liquidated, the survivors were marched to the towns of Voroshilovca, Tivriv and Crasna. In Voroshilovca more than half of them died of hunger or disease.

In 1941 according to Katz, 20,000 Bessarabian Jews were murdered in Bar by the Germans. He saw their skeletons, as well as fragments of documents and luggage, strewn throughout the valley where the massacre took place.[11]

The remaining information about Moghilev department pertains to the plight of a group of deportees in the summer of 1942. On June 14 of that year there arrived in Serebria a group of Czernowitz Jews who had been deported with savage cruelty by Col. Calotescu (*see* page 79). Many had relatives in Moghilev whom they wished to see. The ruthless Gen. Dimitri Stefanescu, however, isolated them completely. They were transported by train to their doom in Ladjin without having exchanged a word with their loved ones.

Six days later the last 450 deportees from Dorohoi arrived in Serebria. Eight months earlier while they worked in Braila, their families had been deported to Moghilev. After being allowed to join them for a tragic reunion, they were sent to Ladjin where their journey and their lives were to end.

Yugastru Department (Vapniarka)

The horrors of Bar testify to the fact that the nearer to Nazi-occupied territory a lager was, the more brutal were the methods used by the Rumanians. The contact with Otto Ohlendorf's and Otto Rasch's *Einsatzgruppen* affected and infected the Rumanians whose attitude toward the Germans in the heyday of Nazi victories was one of abject servility.

In Yugastru Department, situated between Moghilev

and the Bug, was the lager of Vapniarka, a penal camp for communists. Its inmates, who numbered 1,135 in the fall of 1942, were housed in bombed out barracks that had no doors or windows. The new arrivals were greeted by the commander, Col. Ion C. Murgescu: "From here," he would say, "you will go out either on all fours or in a hearse."

He did not exaggerate. He spared nothing in achieving this goal as the indictment against him showed:

> The internees ask for permission to build a water-conduit, he denies it. They beg for permission to make beds of board for the sick, he denies it; to prepare a stove for cooking, he denies it.
>
> The sweltering heat in the summer days! The children clamor for water—in vain. Then Murgescu designs a diabolic trick. He installs a faucet in one of the buildings and announces that henceforth there will be water in abundance. The water starts to drip. Overjoyed, the internees flock to the faucet which suddenly goes dry. The disappointment is terrible, the internees howl in despair . . .

Murgescu fed them a poisonous kind of vegetable whose scientific name is *Lathyrus sativus*. Its consumption leads to indigestion, pains, spasms and finally to partial paralysis. Within three months half of the internees came down with these symptoms. But Murgescu refused to change their menu.

He subjected his victims to corporal punishment. He tried to seduce the women. With the aid of some common criminals who had been placed in this lager he staged a false rebellion and ordered the guards to shoot at the internees. The soldiers refused to obey. "We do not shoot," they demurred. "There is no reason for it. If you want us to shoot, give a written order!"

This sadist and lecher was succeeded by others who were still worse, if possible.

On Oct. 14, 1943 Vapniarka lager was liquidated. A commission was sent from Bucharest to decide the fate of the internees. Those who were found innocent were permitted to return to their homes. Those who were found dangerous elements were transferred to the Targu-Jiu camp. Fifty-two of the internees, communists sentenced to prison terms, were transferred to the Rabnitza prison. At the approach of the Russian armies in March, 1944, they were murdered; by some miracle four of them escaped.

Tulcin Department

This department is situated on the right bank of the Bug. The opposite bank was occupied by Field Marshal Erich Mannstein's armies in whose rear Ohlendorf's henchmen massacred the Jewish population.

In their insatiable, sadistic blood-thirst, *Einsatzgruppe* units frequently entered the camps in this department demanding Jews for destruction. The servile Rumanians surrendered them without hesitation.

The scenes of unbelievable degradation in three of these camps resembled those in Dachau and Bergen-Belsen, whose discovery shocked the civilized world.

PECIORA

Moses Katz reported the following:

Those who succeeded in running away from this camp tell horrible things. It is surrounded by three barbed wire fences. At intervals the Germans come and take

Jews away for execution. The internees having no way
to procure food, eat human excreta and even corpses.[12]

In October and November, 1942, 3,000 Jews from
Moghilev were sent to this place of horror. On Oct. 16
Sgt. Hans Rucker, the chief of a Nazi camp on the other
side of the Bug, required under some pretext all Jewish
girls between 14-20. One hundred and fifty girls were surrendered to him. The beasts took them into a forest, raped
them, and mowed them down with machine guns. One
girl, Frida Koller, escaped to tell the crime. Five weeks
later, 500, and in May 1943, 600 Jews were handed over
to and murdered by the Nazis. On Sept. 1, 1943, 28 Jews
remained alive in Peciora. All the rest had perished.

LADJIN

This place on the banks of the Bug became a mass grave
for Jewish martyrs. To this town and to a nearby quarry
were sent the Jews expelled from Czernowitz in June
1942. Arriving in sealed cattle cars after a five-day journey,
they were taken to the Ladjin Quarry. A few rusty railroad cars, a number of half-ruined barracks—these were
to house the exiles. The deportees, exhausted to the point
of semi-consciousness, were not permitted to occupy their
quarters after their arrival. A pharmacist, Vasilescu, ordered them disinfected. "Here you are mere numbers,"
he shouted. "Here first you starve, then die." He appointed as their chief a Jewish brute named Lederman,
who found a sadistic joy in torturing his brethren.

Of the 4,800 deportees only 1,800 could be crowded into
the existing accommodations. Six hundred were taken to
the town of Ladjin, 600 to Oleanita, and 1,800 to Cetvertinovca. Their fate, however, was the same.

On Aug. 19 the *Todt* organization required 3,000 of these people for work. The prefect of the department, Col. Longhin, was glad to oblige. Having taken them across the Bug, the Germans immediately executed the children and the aged. The able-bodied were put to work and gradually, as they became incapacitated, executed.

Of the original number of Ladjin deportees only 1,800 remained—400 in the quarry, 78 in Oleanita and 1,000 in Cetvertinovca.

On Aug. 26 the quarry was evacuated. Half of the inmates were sent to the town of Ladjin, the other half to Cetvertinovca. Sixty insane were detained and killed in the quarry. Two days later the Jews sent to Ladjin were returned to the quarry. Their fate is unknown. On Sept. 1, 1943, there was not a single Jew either in the quarry or in the town of Ladjin.

THE CITY OF TULCIN

The city of Tulcin is the capital of Tulcin Department. In its vicinity a turbine was built at the cost of Jewish sweat and blood. Thousands of deportees were brought here from Moghilev, Bershad and other ghettos. From dawn to dusk, the undernourished prisoners stood knee-deep in mud and mire, driven by brutal guards until the last drop of their strength was gone. The places of those who succumbed were immediately filled with new groups of Jews. The number of the victims (not officially established) ran into the thousands.

This department was also a hunting ground of the murderous *Einsatzgruppen*. The prefects surrendered Jews for the asking. For a while the exiles were unaware of what their surrender meant; they could not imagine that men should be murdered for no reason at all. At the beginning the unsuspecting Jews who volunteered for transfer to the other bank of the Bug, were hopeful of better treatment by the Germans. But soon the awful truth revealed itself.

On Aug. 2, 1943, Poiana Volbura, the prefect and a poet of note, handed 200 Jews over to the Nazis. The victims were beguiled into thinking that they were assigned to work at the turbine. On the way they discovered that they were marching to their death. This did not impress them in the least; after years of deprivation and degradation they were resigned to die. But they sought to save the 52 children who were among them. They bribed the guards who released the children. The little ones found their way back to Tulcin. When they arrived the next day in the ghetto, hungry, ragged, vermin-filled creatures, most of them were orphans.

Berezovca Department

This department is the cemetery of 30,000 Odessa Jews and of many thousands of native (Ukrainian) Jews. During the winter of 1941-42 the Rumanians evacuated the Odessa-Slobodnik ghetto and sent the inmates to various places in this department.

Units of Ohlendorf's bloodhounds were stationed in this region. Immediately after the evacuees' arrival the German henchmen subjected them to "special treatment"—facts corroborated by report series of the head of the Odessa Police.

The graves of these martyrs are scattered throughout the department. Here are the places of their execution: Mustovoi, Vasilievo, Cihrin, Hulievca, Catovsca, Lisinovca, Bernandovca, Suha-Verba.

Balta Department

BERSHAD

In this city, the second largest center of the deportees, the treatment of the Jews was barbarous. For the privilege of staying in the city, the pretor, Constantin Alexandrescu, extorted 10,000 Lei for each person. Those unable to pay were dispersed to the small towns (Bandizovca —116 inmates, Voitcovca—893, Ushtea—945, Tibulovca—390, in September, 1943).

Pretor Alexandrescu together with a cousin of his launched a reign of terror, beating, torturing, terrorizing the Jews for no reason whatever. He forbade the Jews to sell their clothing, their only means of getting food. Infractors were punished, and their food confiscated.

The desperate situation was mitigated when a decent man, Lieut. Gheorghe Petrescu, was appointed commander of the lager. But the government would not tolerate humane administration. A year later he was replaced by a brute, Lieut. Gheorghe Grigorescu.

The typhus epidemic did not bypass Bershad and its vicinity. As in Obodovca, nothing was and could be done to combat it. Before winter's end in 1942 more than half of the 20,000 exiles were dead. In Ushtea alone 1,600 of the 2,500 Jews died. In the sub-zero weather they could not be buried in the rock-like, frozen ground; their corpses lay around for weeks.

TZIBULOVCA

Two thousand persons were herded here into a miserable overcrowded building. When the typhus epidemic was over their number was 180 (100 men, 76 women, 4 children).

BUDI

The same fate awaited the 1,200 deportees here. Their vast majority was wiped out by the epidemic. Among the victims was the famous Storojinetzer rabbi together with the ten members of his family.

OBODOVCA

The inmates were driven from the inferno of Marculesti to find a possibly worse inferno here. They were put up in stables and were permitted to buy food only with jewels, gold, silver.

In June 1943, 1,560 Jews were sent from Obodovca to Nikolaev, the headquarters of *Einsatzgruppe* D. That was their end.

It appears a miracle that on Sept. 1, 1943, there were still 1,373 Jews living in Obodovca.

780 of them were transferred to Luhova.

LUHOVA

The mayor greeted the deportees with: "Here will be your graves." They were locked up in stables together with the cattle. Once in two days they were allowed to go out for water and food. Typhus raged here as furiously as it had in Bershad.

The ghettos were declared as contaminated and surrounded with barbed wire. No one was permitted to leave them. Many died, not of the disease but of hunger.

Throughout the winter the dead lay buried in the high snow. In April the Jews collected and interred them in mass graves.

Golta Department

The largest of the Transnistrian cemeteries, Golta contains the ashes of the 48,000 Jews killed and their corpses burned at Bogdanovca, the graves of 12,000 Jews shot to death at Dumanovca, and the resting places of 4,000 Jews starved and tortured to death at Acmecetca (the work of that Rumanian monster, Modest Isopescu and his worthy deputy, Aristide Padure. *See* Chap. 3.)

All these were Soviet Jews. Of the Rumanian exiles, there remained 874 persons alive on Sept. 1, 1943.

Oceacov Department

Near the town of Trihatz a mile-long bridge was constructed under the supervision of a German engineer named Neumayer. This sadist treated the Jewish slave laborers in strict adherence to the Nazi extermination-through-work principles. Upon their arrival the Jews were counted by strokes with leather lashes. They lived in stables with wet walls. They had to work 14-15 hours a day.

After the day's exacting toil Neumayer subjected them to additional tortures. He would line them up in two rows facing each other, and at a given signal they had to beat their opposite numbers. The mutual beating had to be real. German soldiers stood behind the victims and bore down upon whoever spared his fellow man.

The daily food ration was a plate of barley soup and 200 grams of bread. The undernourished slave laborers wore rags or wrapped their nakedness in newspapers. Whatever aid was sent to them was robbed by the Germans.

Jews were killed for the slightest offenses, such as stepping out of the dormitory by night.

On Sept. 1, 1943, the number of the inmates was 608.

6

The Extermination of the Native (Soviet) Jews of Transnistria

Before the outbreak of the German-Soviet war approximately 300,000 Jews lived in the southern corner of Soviet Ukraine between the Pruth and the Bug, an area which the Rumanians named Transnistria. How many of them fled to Soviet Russia before the onslaught of the German-Rumanian forces? This is a highly controversial issue. Soviet sources asserted that the vast majority of the Jews was systematically evacuated. They reported among other things that "the entire population left Odessa prior to the city's occupation."[1]

Joseph Schechtman believes that "despite the (Russian) Army's urgent need for transportation thousands of trains were provided for evacuation."[2] Others share this optimistic view and believe that " . . . the bulk of the Jews of . . . Soviet Russia's Jews escaped to the interior . . . also a very large proportion of the Jews of the annexed territories."[3]

But both Solomon M. Schwartz in his *The Jews in the Soviet Union* and the Special Report of the Select Committee of the House of Representatives take a different position. "Pro-Soviet propagandists disseminated the legend that the Soviet government made special efforts to save the Jews from the Nazis. A careful analysis of all

119

available data shows that . . . no such measures were taken."

Odessa

On Oct. 16, 1941, the Rumanian troops entered the city of Odessa which only a few decades ago, at the time of Achad Haam and his followers, was one of the great centers of Jewish culture and literature.

Upon their entry into the city, the occupying forces killed a number of innocent citizens, among them many a Jew.[4] Six days later a delayed-action land mine destroyed the headquarters of the Rumanian army and killed the commander, Gen Glogojeanu, 16 officers, 35 soldiers and nine sergeants.

Although an investigation by Gen. Jacobici immediately established that the mine had been planted by the retreating enemy,[5] Ion Antonescu decided to follow the Nazi pattern set a few days earlier at a similar event in Minsk.[6] He ordered 200 communists killed for every officer and 100 for every soldier. Immediately throughout the city men and women were seized and hanged on gallows. Others were shot to death. The number of victims was about 5,000.

Yet this did not satiate the blood-crazed Rumanians. On Oct. 23, thousands upon thousands of the population were herded into the jails. The next morning an endless crowd was driven to the city limits. There were four storehouses in the Dalnic section, into which the victims were squeezed and locked up. Then breaches were cut in the buildings' walls and machine guns were placed in them. At a given sign the guns opened fire, wounding and killing the shouting, howling, hapless crowd.

"But the henchmen did not think this method efficient

enough—long rows of doomed men were waiting outside for their execution. The operation had to be sped up. It was about 5 P.M., and in October it started to get dark . . . So they flooded the buildings with gasoline and set them aflame."[7]

Hell broke loose and, as night descended, the sights and sounds of masses of men, women and children burning alive defied description.

"Some of those inside appeared at the windows pointing at their head or heart for a bullet—the moment the soldiers raised their rifles to shoot, the victims disappeared. Then they reappeared ready to die. Women in an effort to save their children threw them out the window. There they were shot dead by the soldiers. One child with hands uplifted was seen running around for ten minutes—most soldiers had no heart to shoot at him."[8]

Twenty to thirty thousand Jews were executed in this manner under the order of Ion Antonescu in whose house "no chickens were killed." At his trial this coward dared to assert that he had never heard of these acts of barbarism until two years later.

The remaining Jews of Odessa, about 40,000, were segregated in a ghetto. They were released on Nov. 3 and then segregated again on Nov. 11

Bogdanovca, Dumanovca, Acmecetca

In order to see the situation clearly, we must emphasize that after the conclusion of the deportations, there were two groups of Jews living in Transnistria: Jews deported from Rumania proper and Bessarabia; and the local, Ukrainian Jews.

Decree No. 23 ordered that all local Jews had to be

removed into concentration camps. Only a few Ukrainian Jews were exempted from this ordeal. In Moghilev, 3,733; in Shargorod, about 2,000; in Rabnita, 1,467; in Tulcin, 118; and in Spicov, 27 local Jews could stay. The rest of the local Jews met a swift and terrible end.

The department of Golta was assigned as the site for their concentration. In Bogdanovca, there were concentrated 48,000 Ukrainian Jews; in Dumanovca, 18,000; and in Acmecetca, 4,000.

The prefect of this department was Col. Modest Isopescu, a sadistic monster, whose aide, Aristide Padure, was worthy of him. These beasts with human faces, as their indictment calls them, decided to exterminate all the internees.

In Bogdanovca 48,000 men were massacred in the days preceding Christmas.

On December 21, early in the morning, they took out of the lager the invalid, the sick, and those of the women who, after weeks of starvation, were unable to march. They were herded into stables which were flooded with kerosene and set afire.

In these buildings 4,500-5,000 people were burned alive. The remaining 43,000 persons were sent to a nearby woods and while the buildings and the victims were still burning, the vast mass of men realized that this was their death-march . . . The scenes that developed were terrible—mothers lifted their children heavenward, beseeching God for mercy; other parents, on the contrary, encouraged their children to face death with firmness and calm . . .

Arriving in the desert first they were robbed of all. Then they were ordered to undress, whereafter groups of 300-400 were formed and murdered with grenades. Thus it went on until Christmas. On December 24th the massacre was suspended; that same day Isopescu came and took pictures of the scene. On Dec. 28-29, the bloody work was continued and finished."

Two hundred robust men were left alive to burn the corpses. This job took two months; at the end of it, 150 of them were executed.[9]

In destroying 48,000 men in four days, Isopescu set a record unrivalled not only by Ohlendorf, Kube and other S. S. leaders, but even by the German death factories of Maidanek or Auschwitz.

This monster cannot be accused of lack of ingenuity. In the extermination of the other lagers he used different methods.

At Dumanovca there were 18,000 Jews concentrated. In order to prolong their sufferings he ordered that at the interval of 3-4 days groups of 300-400 should be killed. Thus the process of extermination was dragged through the months of January and February.

. . . at Acmecetca the 4,000 people were exterminated by hunger. This lager was located in a *kolhoz* far away from any human settlement. Isopescu isolated it perfectly and prohibited the shipping there of any food. After days of starvation the entirely exhausted inmates were given raw potatoes. Whereafter raw maize-flour was distributed among them. The hunger-crazed inmates devoured whatever they were given, with the result that their bellies puffed up and they died amidst terrible pains.[10]

This lager with its starving and desperate population was often visited by Isopescu. This sadist and drunkard would watch his victims; he enjoyed their agony, took pictures of their tortured writhings and sent them to the Bucharest papers.[11]

In the midst of all these acts of horror, Alexianu issued

another decree (Jan. 18, 1942) ordering that the still un-deported Jews be concentrated in Slobodka, a section of Odessa. In the arctic cold of the Russian winter these un-fortunates had to leave their homes. But they found no rest in Slobodka. They were thence sent to Vasilievo, in Berezovca Department. Groups of 1,000-2,000 were shipped daily to that valley of death. Their sufferings were frightful.

Police Col. Broshteanu reported the following:

> Because of the cold which often sinks to 20° Celsius below zero and of undernourishment, many fall on the road and freeze (after their arrival while marching to the lager).
> The police have to be exchanged daily because of the unbearable cold.[12]

Many of the exiles committed suicide.

Ohlendorf's units were stationed in Berezovca Depart-ment. These murderers entered the lagers as soon as the exiles arrived and finished them off. Col. Broshteanu re-ports that in Cihrin the German police shot to death 772 "interned" Jews and that on Mar. 13, 1942 a unit of 16 S. S. men executed 650 Jews.[13] Report after report con-veys similar information.

About 30,000 Odessa Jews who survived the massacres and death-by-fire of October 23-24 and not less than 10,000 Jews from the neighboring departments were transferred to and executed in the various lagers of Berezovca Depart-ment.[14] These facts are documented by a series of police reports and by the Central Office of the Rumanian Jews. On Mar. 22, 1943 a delegation of that office visited Odessa and found a total of 60 Jews in the city.

These are the facts. The Jews deported to Berezovca

were not distributed among the Rumanian Jews and subsequently brought back to Odessa as many have assumed. They were murdered.[15]

Within a half year between Oct. 16, 1941 and April, 1942, approximately 132,000 local Jews who had resided between the Pruth and Bug were destroyed—92,000 at the hand of the Rumanians, (22,000 in Odessa, 48,000 in Bogdanovca, 18,000 in Dumanovca, and 4,000 in Acmecetca) , 40,000 by the Germans.

7

Relief, Repatriation and Rescue Efforts

Troubled times bring forth the highest and lowest types of men—heroes who give their lives to save others on the one hand and despicable traitors on the other hand.

The name of "Avocat Shapiro" (no additional data) of Kishinev who after a fantastic flight to Bucharest on behalf of his brethren chose to return to perish with them; the names of the Moghilev and Shargarod physicians, who during the epidemic sacrificed themselves in the hospitals; the name of that undaunted champion and defender of his brethren, William Filderman, shall never be forgotten.

However, there were also some dark figures, scoundrels of the lowest order among the Jews. One of them was Dr. N. Ghingold, the president of the Central Office of the Rumanian Jews.

Following the Nazi pattern, Ion Antonescu dissolved the national organizations, the true representatives of the country's Jewry (UER, the Federation of the Synagogues) and set up a central office led by cringing cowards who betrayed their fellows for personal benefits. Nowhere was Ghingold's attitude more repulsive than in matters of relief for the deportees.

> From the very outset . . . Dr. Ghingold assumed the position that any action on behalf of the deportees had to be abandoned since the very idea of it was not agree-

able to the government; the government considered
them as the enemies of the country and they should be
regarded as such by the Jews. Whoever assumed the
work of aiding the deportees would assume highly
serious personal risks and responsibilities. As far as he
was concerned, he regarded his competence as termi-
nated at the Prut (the border of Transnistria), nothing
that was beyond it was of his concern.

This attitude was, of course, not shared by the real leaders of Jewry. As a result of their labors on Dec. 10, 1941,
a decree authorized the Central Office (originally the Federation of Synagogues that soon after was dissolved) to
send aid to the deportees. This was regarded as an achieve-
ment of the first order in these apocalyptic days when the
official policy envisaged not the preservation but the annihilation of Jewish lives.

Dr. M. Zimmer, a personal friend of Mihai Antonescu,
took matters in his own hands and formed within the
framework of the Central Office a relief committee composed of himself and of A. Schwefelberg, Fred Sharaga,
and Dr. E. Kostiner.

Dr. Ghingold had to accept this situation. But he reserved for himself the right to supervise and sign the committee's correspondence. He used his right to the full. In
some cases letters had to wait for weeks for his signature.
This policy of procrastination considerably hampered the
committee's actions and cost Jewish lives in Transnistria.

The relief committee appealed to the Jews of Rumania
for money and supplies. The response could not be expected to be generous since the Jews had been pauperized
by the various "Rumanization" decrees. They had to surrender part of their clothing to help the war efforts, to
make heavy contributions toward a national war loan, and

in addition, to pay as ransom the exorbitant amount of 4-billion Leis ($8,000,000).

In connection with the ransom, it was decided that a 15% special tax should be added to it for the aid of the deportees. Thus 110 million Leis was collected for the work of charity, but the unprincipled Dr. Ghingold released only 16,626,000 Leis for that purpose.

Under the circumstances, the work of the Relief Committee deserves admiration.

The sent to the lagers:

Cash	79,462,000 Leis
Cash to individuals	81,669,000 "
Food	24,000,000 "
Medicine	14,458,000 "
	199,589,000 Leis
	(Approximately $400,000)

Clothing valued at 270,844,500 Leis ($540,000), was sent as well as hundreds of tons of salt, coal, window glass, lumber, rope, nails, shovels and various tools for craftsmen.

During the same period another relief committee was formed, composed of Berthold Sobel, Salo Schmidt, and others. Its treasurer was a gentile, Traian Pocopovici, who worked underground to raise the equivalent of $200,000. They supported both the Transnistrian exiles as well as the paupers in Czernowitz.

The amounts sent by the American Jewish organizations were, in comparison a pittance—25,000,000 Leis ($50,000).

In October 1942 Wilhelm Fisher, the representative of the World Jewish Congress in Rumania, got in touch with Saby Mayer, the representative of the American Joint Distribution Committee and Dr. Silberschein of the World Jewish Congress, both in Switzerland.

After months of communication, a Swiss journalist, Hans Welti, offered his services to the committee as mediator between Bucharest and Geneva. Whenever he travelled to Switzerland, he took with him and brought back correspondence and financial instructions. At the beginning of 1944, the Bucharest leaders were arrested. Their accuser was their trusted mediator Welti, who, it turns out, was a spy for the Gestapo.

Fortunately Prime Minister Mihai Antonescu, ordered them released after six weeks of detention. He had just returned from a visit to Rome where he came to the conclusion that the Axis had lost the war. Therefore, he sought to build up an alibi for his non-implication. Nevertheless, Welti's exposé put an end to the work in this country of the American organizations.

A noble gesture of the Pope has to be mentioned here. In February 1944, he transmitted the amount of 1,353,000 Leis ($2,500) toward the aid of the Jewish deportees.

The Rumanian political leaders are known for their sagacity and astuteness. Centuries of oppression at the hand of the Turks, Russians and the Greek fanariots taught them the art of swimming with and not against the tide. They know a change in the situation if they see one and are quick to jump on the right bandwagon before it is too late.

Hitler's first victories stupefied them, like many others. But at the end of 1942 the Nazis' march of triumph was definitely halted. The British offensive at El Alamein, the landing of the American troops in North Africa, the Stalingrad disaster shook their belief in the Nazis' invincibility. The political climate changed, and the government's attitude toward the Jews changed with it.

At the end of October 1942, an interministerial committee was formed in order "to regulate and coordinate" the legislation concerning the treatment of the Jews. Its deliberations already reflected the new official attitude. When on Nov. 24, a motion was made for new deportations, the committee unanimously rejected it. At its next meeting, the committee discussed a surprisingly new subject—the repatriation of the exiled Jews!

The Jewish leaders did their utmost to rescue their brethren. During his exile in 1943 in Moghilev, Dr. Filderman submitted a memorandum to the government demanding on the basis of his own experiences the repatriation of the deportees. Dr. Ghingold, true to his treacherous self, instead of promoting, sought to hinder and foil these efforts.

It took a year and a half for the new policy to bear its first fruits. The obstacles were twofold. First, the shifting mood of Ion Antonescu who, like Penelope of old, was prone to undo by night all that had been accomplished by day. Time and again he refused to sign measures to which he previously had agreed. The second obstacle was the iron fist of the Gestapo. These terrorists demanded an exorbitant ransom for permitting the emigration of the Jews from Rumania.

There were two periods of the rescue efforts.

Emigration

On Nov. 22, 1942, the Commissar of Jewish Affairs, Radu Lecca, notified the Jewish leaders of the government's willingness to permit the emigration of the 75,000 deportees in Transnistria for a ransom of billions of Leis (tens of millions of dollars).

Nothing came of this project as no country was willing to offer even temporary haven to Jewish refugees. The only logical place, Palestine, was closed by Great Britain, whose government would not offend the susceptibilities of the Arabs.

In these conditions, the Jewish leaders adopted a realistic policy. They strove to repatriate:

a. the 5,000 orphans in Transnistria whose misery was indescribable.

b. the 6,430 Jews from Dorohoi Department (their original number was 10,368) on the ground that their deportation had been an administrative error.

c. those deported for minor infractions of the forced labor decrees.

d. those who had been exiled without satisfactory grounds to the horror camp of Vapniarka.

e. the 578 Jews deported for having applied in 1940 for settlement in Soviet Russia.

In January 1943, the government permitted the emigration of the orphans. For this, however, the approval of the Gestapo was necessary. Dr. Filderman contacted Killinger's friend, Dr. A. Tessler, who promised his cooperation for a consideration of $3,000 (originally $40,000).

Now Dr. Filderman applied to the large Jewish organizations abroad for visas—the granting of which the Western powers flatly refused.

Return to Rumania

Now the Jewish leaders concentrated their efforts upon bringing the orphans back into the country. They applied for a permit to repatriate all the 5,000 orphans, those deprived of both parents as well as those who had lost one of them. Dr. Ghingold recommended the repatriation of only those who had lost both parents.

On Nov. 12, 1943, the International Commission's decision reflected Ghingold's wishes; at the beginning of 1944 it announced that it would permit the return of about 2,500 orphans.

On Mar. 6, 1944, a group of 1,846 orphans arrived in the City of Jassy where they were distributed among the various congregations.

In the same decision of Nov. 12, 1943, the interministerial commission approved the repatriation of the Dorohoi Jews. Five weeks later they began their journey back to their homes. But even at the last moments they were subjected to indignities and acts of extortion by the authorities.

In the course of 1943, two commissions from Bucharest screened the inmates in Vapniarka on their future detention or release. The second commission recommended that 218 be sent home, 209 be released to live in Transnistria, and 127 be retained in Vapniarka. The governor of Transnistria, however, decided that no one should return to Rumania proper; he interned the first two categories in three Transnistrian towns. After many interventions they were permitted to return to their homes in January, 1944. The other 563 Vapniarka inmates were transferred to the Targu-Jiu lager in the country. But 50 internees, avowed communists, were sent to prison in Rabnita where the night of Mar. 18 they were massacred a few hours before the arrival of the Russian troops.

The 568 deportees who had opted for Russia could not be repatriated. Except for 16 they all had been killed immediately after their arrival in Transnistria. The survivors were repatriated at the end of 1943 from the city of Tighina together with 56 other deportees.

In the spring of 1944, Ion Antonescu no longer had doubts as to the outcome of the war. Brooding over the map he would say to his intimate, the Chief of the Secret police, "Look here, Cristescu, this isn't a front, this is a catastrophe."[1]

Now, at this belated hour, with the chill of disaster in his bones, he sought, even as Himmler did a year later,[2] to improve his records.

Rescinding his decree of Jan. 27, 1944, which prohibited the repatriation of the deportees, on Mar. 14 he ordered all the deported Jews repatriated.

It was too late. The big Russian offensive which had started on March 10 at Uman had swept within ten days across the entire territory of Transnistria.

One Jewish committee which left Bucharest with a view to repatriating the exiles in Moghilev could no longer reach the city.

Another rescue committee succeeded in reaching Balta and bringing 2,518 deportees back into the country. They were all permitted to return into their homes except for the 563 Vapniarka inmates who were interned in Targu-Jiu.

Here are the results of the rescue efforts:

Orphans repatriated	1,846
Jews from Dorohoi repatriated	1,500
Survivors of those who opted for Russia, et. al.	70
Repatriated from Balta	2,518
Repatriated from Vapniarka	410
(17 of the 427 were detained)	
	6,344 persons

8

The Forgotten Cemetery:
the Grim Statistics

Transnistria became the cemetery of more than 200,000 Rumanian and Russian Jews. We shall now present in detail the gruesome statistics of this dark chapter of our age.

On the basis of the Rumanian censuses of 1930,[1] of Apr. 6, 1941,[2] and of May 20, 1942,[3] the number of Jews in Bukovina and Bessarabia may be stated to have been 301,886 in 1930. In 1940 their number was somewhat, but not considerably, smaller.[4] A fraction of this group fled with the retreating Russians, others were massacred, and the rest were deported, except for some 16,000 Jews in Czernowitz.[5] Deportations proceeded in three waves: Sept. 12 to Nov. 10, 1941; Oct. 9 to Dec. 31, 1941; and the period following.

Immediately after the outbreak of the Russo-German phase of World War II on June 22, 1941, the Jews of Bessarabia (except those from Kishinev) and of North Bukovina (i.e., the northern segment of the Department of Radautz and the whole Department of Storojinetz, except for the city of Storojinetz) were uprooted and concentrated in three camps in Bessarabia. Between Sept. 12 through Nov. 10, 1941, they were deported from Bessarabia to Transnistria (the first wave). A new census taken before their deportation indicated that there were 54,028 Jews in the camps of Edinetz, Secureni, and Vertujeni.[6]

During the period of the second wave, the Jews of

Kishinev, of the City and Department of Czernowitz, and of South Bukovina (Departments Suceava, Campulung, South Radautz, and Dorohoi) were deported. About 10,-400 were removed from the Kishinev ghetto.[7] Out of a Jewish population of 49,500 in the City and Department of Czernowitz,[8] about 29,500 were deported.[9] The city of Storojinetz deported two thousand Jews;[10] from the Jewish population of the Department of Suceava, Radautz, and Campulung, totaling 18,180,[11] 17,961 were removed along with 11,547 from the Dorohoi Department.[12]

The last deportations included 4,000 Jews from Czernowitz in June 1942;[13] 1,046 deported from Targu-Jiu, from jails and other places to Camp Vapniarka;[14] 1,172 deported for other reasons.[15] To these must be added the 8,500 victims of the 25,000 marched to Transnistria by the Rumanians on July 25, 1941, but driven back by the Germans on Aug. 17, 1941.[16] The cumulative total of all deported during this period was 140,154.

It must be pointed out, however, that the real number of the deportees was considerably larger. It is impossible to determine, even approximately, the thousands who in the interval before June 22 to Sept. 12, 1941, perished in the camps of Edinetz, Secureni, and Vartujeni, as well as the hundreds who had been shot on their way from these camps to "points of transfer."

On Sept. 16, 1943, the General Inspectorate of the Rumanian Gendarmerie submitted to the Rumanian Ministry of Internal Affairs a detailed report on the Transnistrian camps,[17] describing the situation as of Sept. 1, 1943. It must be kept in mind that during the seven months between the date of this report and the liberation on March 20, 1944, a number of the exiles died. Others, like the Jewish partisans in Barshad and a number of the Vapniarka inmates, were murdered. Nor did the report give a full picture of the number of deportees and casualties in preceding months.[18]

However, the data of the gendarmerie report can conservatively be accepted. They indicate that there were 50,741 survivors in various Transnistrian camps[19] and 1,656 survivors in the Vapniarka camp, a total of 52,397.[20] Having ascertained that 140, 154 had been deported,[21] the conclusion is inevitable: 87,757 deportees perished, all of them from Rumania. Of the *local* Jewish population, the data show that 130,000 died the death of martyrs; 20,000 from Odessa,[22] 48,000 in Bogdanovca, 18,000 in Dumanovca, 4,000 in Acmecetca[23] and 40,000 in the Berezovca Department by henchmen of S.S. Maj. General Otto Ohlendorf.[24] *Thus a total of 217,757 were annihilated in that vast cemetery which was Transnistria.*

Having determined the number of victims in Transnistria, it now remains to fix the responsibility for these crimes.

Of those deported to Transnistria, the Germans murdered in Bar 12,000;[25] in Garisin 1,230;[26] in Ladjin 3,000;[27] in Rastadt 1,000;[28] in Peciora 1,250;[29] in Mustovoi 120;[30] and 200 in Tulcin[31]—a total of 18,800. In addition, they murdered 40,000 local (Soviet) Jews, bringing the total to 58,800 in this area. They also murdered a large but unidentified number of Bessarabia Jews in Scazinetz.[32]

A total of 87,757 Rumanian Jews perished, of whom the Germans destroyed 18,800. This means, then, that the Rumanians destroyed 68,957 of their own Jewish countrymen. As they annihilated 70,000 local Soviet Jews, it is clear that the Rumanians exterminated 138,957 Jews in Transnistria alone.

Reference to German pressure will not absolve Antonescu and his henchmen of their guilt nor mitigate their crime. One need only to point to the attitude of Bulgaria,

Denmark, and Finland whose heroic resistance saved their Jewish populations from a similar fate. Thus, while the total responsibility rests with the National Socialist government of Germany, the regime of Antonescu must stand as an ignominious accomplice to history's most horrendous crime.[33]

Notes for Introduction

Notes (For abbreviations *see Bibliography*.)
1 *C. N. page 13.*
2 *P.M.T.*, Testimonies of Iuliu Maniu, Dinu Bratianu. Gheorghe Bratianus.

Chapter 1

1 Greek publicans or tax-collectors who hailed from Fanar, a suburb of Istanbul.
2 Dr. M. Broszat, *Das Dritte Reich und Rumanische Judenpolitik*, Munich 1957 (multigraphed) slavishly follows Ion Gheorghe *page 33*, forgetful of the fact that Germany with her perfectly assimilated Jews has been the breeding ground of anti-Semitism, while in Czechoslovakia, despite the large masses of non-assimilated Jews, anti-Semitism was almost non existent.
3 Nicholae Iorga, "Istoria Evreilor din Tarile noastre," quoted in *A.E., page 5.*
4 Elbogen, *pages 68, 356.* (Ion Gheorghe, *op. cit.*, often refers to this fact.)
5 Elbogen, *op. cit., page 358.* As early as 1891, 39% of all pupils were Jewish until the government limited their number.
6 *P.E., page 109,* shows that the percentage of Jewish physicians was 24.8% while the percentage of the Jews in the total population was 1.9%.
7 Hillgruber, *page 5.*
8 *Ibid., pages 11–12.*
9 Hillgruber, *page 268,* footnote 1, on the basis of Fabricius' information.
10 According to Gheorghe his ideal seemed to be Kaiser Wilhelm II. The same nervous agitation, the same lack of perseverance, the same proclivity for pomp and autocracy, the same plan—forging and occupation with trifles. Carol was intelligent, but his character was weak.

11 During World War I he married Mme. Zizi Lambrino who bore him a son. He later divorced her to marry Princess Helena, the daughter of King Constantine of Greece; with her he fathered Mihai I. Then he took as his mistress Magda Lupescu, a Jewess and the wife of an officer. In 1925 when his father, King Ferdinand, sought to prevail on him to break with her, he decided to renounce the throne and leave the country. When Carol returned five years later he brought Mme. Lupescu back with him to his "Palat" thus breaking the pledge he had made to Iuliu Maniu to restore his legal marriage to Queen Elena. Magda soon became his nemesis. Obstinate and vengeful, she plunged the king into conflicts with all of his political leaders. Finally he remained alone.

12 *P.M.T., page 155 ff.*

13 Hillgruber, *page 9.*

14 *Ibid., page 11.*

15 *P.M.T., page 155, ff.*

16 Hillgruber, *page 13.*

17 Gheorghe, *page 31,* acknowledges that "the tender plant of the Legionary Movement drew its vital forces" from the support of the fascist, nationalist revolution.

18 *P.M.T., page 173,* Cristescu at his trial stated that the actual number was 800,000. However, Hillgruber, *page 260,* gives the official statistics as follows: The Liberal Party, 36%; the National Peasant Party, 20%; The Iron Guard, 16%; the Christian-National Party of Goga-Cuza, 8%.

19 *P.M.T., page 173.*

20 *Ibid., page 174.*

21 Gheorghe, *pages 31–5.*

22 Gafencu, *Vorspiel, pages 305–8;* Hillgruber, *pages 12–13* follows their appraisal uncritically.

23 The prosecutor at his trial on May 27, 1938 described him as a man of low intellectual capacities who would sit for hours idly dawdling with his fingers.

24 His was a rather primitive brand of mysticism, if it can even be termed as such. His party's propaganda seems to be a collection of the phrases typical of those preached in any village church by a "popa" of the Greco-Oriental Church. For example, in an article entitled "Rumanian Messianism" published in *Guarda,* the organ of the Legionnaire movement, Camp Muscel, Dec. 1, 1940, we read:

As far as their structure is concerned there is no difference between racism, Hitlerism and communism. All
three are mystic movements with human objectives.

But the Legionnaire Movement represents for the
first time in modern history a collective spiritual movement because only this movement rises to God.
This movement is, first of all, faith in God, in its
purest sense, in the spirit of our Christian tradition.

And in excerpts from a pamphlet entitled "From the
World of the Legionary Movement," (published by the
same periodical), we find:

As far as peoples are concerned the 'Capitan' says that
their goal is not any type of life but resurrection. The
resurrection of the peoples in the name of Jesus. The
time will come when all nations will rise from death
with all their dead and all kings and their kingdoms,
each having its place before the Lord. This is the highest
goal to which a Nation can rise.

25 *Hitler's Ten-Year War, page 81.*
26 *P.M.T., pages 136–139.*
27 This analysis seems to be borne out by an open letter
written by a dissident pioneer of the Iron Guard, Mihail
Stelescu, and quoted in *Sange si Lacrimi* (Blood and
Tears), Cleveland, Ohio, 1942, *pages 8–14,* originally published in *Cruciada Romanismului* (The Rumanian Cru-
sade), Bucharest, April 4, 1935.
  Stelescu repeatedly states that Codreanu *was built up
into a myth.* He accuses the "Capitan" of dissoluteness,
participation in bachannals held in convents, of using the
Party's treasury for his own purposes.
  On July 16, 1936, nine Iron Guardists invaded the
Bucharest hospital where Stelescu was a patient and killed
him with 120 shots and "dismembering him danced wildly
around the bloody limbs." *(Ibid., page 14.)*
28 Premier Goga's negotiations with the Legionnaires concerning holding new elections and forming a coalition
government precipitated his forced resignation. Also the
English and French governments protested his anti-Jewish
laws. (Hillgruber, *pages 15–16; Unity in Dispersion,
pages 97–101,* gives a brief account of the feverish efforts

of this organization in order to bring about these protests and interventions.

29 Hillgruber, *pages 16–17.*

30 Gafencu, *page 302.*

31 Hillgruber, *pages 25–26.* Chamberlain not only refused to send a delegation for the purpose of intensifying the economic connections between their two countries, he also denied Rumania credit to buy weapons in Britain.

32 *Ibid., pages 27–28.*

33 Hillgruber, *page 29.* They assassinated the rector of the Cluj University.

34 Hillgruber, *page 46 ff.*

35 *Ibid., page 56.*

36 *Ibid., page 75 ff.*

37 *P.M.T. page 227.*

38 Gheorghe, *page 23.*

39 Hillgruber, *page 16.* At Codreanu's trial on May 27, 1938, he testified in his favor.

40 Hillgruber, *page 14; P.M.T., page 5.*

41 Gheorghe, *page 3.* A small, rugged region near Jassy where King Decebal fell in action.

42 *Ibid., page 38*

43 Gheorghe's chronology on *page 43* is misleading, muddled and superficial.

44 There are various versions as to what happened on those two fateful days. According to Iuliu Maniu's testimony before the People's Court of Justice (*P.M.T. page 201*) the political leaders mutually pledged themselves not to cooperate with the king and to demand his abdication. Then Antonescu broke his pledge and accepted his appointment as premier from the king.

Hillgruber, *pages 93–4,* states that Dr. Fabritius played a pivotal role in the developments. When Antonescu informed him of his failure to form a government and of his intention to give up his undertaking, Fabritius advised him to demand full powers from the king, and then to use them to force his abdication. Antonescu did so.

Gheorghe's account (*page 58*) about Antonescu's bold last-minute action is not supported by fact.

45 *Bloodbath in Rumania,* "The Record," published by the United Rumanian Jews of America, New York, 1942, Vol. IV, *page 22.* Prof. Iorga, the famous scholar and poet was an anti-Semite. Some altercation with Codreanu drew the

ire of the Legionnaires on his head. He paid the extreme penalty at the hand of his own diciples.

46 *Ibid., page 36.*
47 "Hitler's Ten-Year War on the Jews," *page 87.*
48 *Bloodbath in Rumania, page 36.*
49 *P.M.T., page 175.*
50 *Ibid., pages 49–50.*
51 *Ibid., page 270.*
52 *Ibid., page 254.*
53 *Ibid., page 29.*
54 *Ibid., pages 259, 242, 30.*
55 *Trei Ani de Guvernare.*
56 *P.M.T., page 30.*
57 Hillgruber, *pages 118–19.*
58 *Hitler's Secret Service, page 114.* (This is the same Heydrich whose assassination caused the extermination of Lidice.)
59 *P.M.T., pages 11, 269.*
60 Hillgruber, *pages 120–1.*
61 Gheorghe, *page 222.*
62 In his reply to Ingeneer H. Clelan, on Feb. 4, 1944, who had interceded with him on behalf of the repatriation of the deportees, he said: "I was determined to deport all Jews from Bukovina and Bessarabia. Yielding to various interventions and petitions I did not do it. I regret that I did not do it." He continued with a flood of wild accusations against the miserable deportees. *C.N., pages 458–9.*

Chapter 2

1 *P.M.T., page 93.*
2 *Ibid., page 50.*
3 *P.M.T., pages 34, 303; C.N., page 92.*
4 *P.M.T., page 34.*
5 *C.N., page 91.*
6 *Ibid., page 46.*
7 *Ibid., page 27.*
8 *Ibid., page 29.*
9 *Ibid., pages 30, 77.*
10 *Ibid., page 31.*
11 *Ibid., page 77.*

12 *Ibid., pages 31–32.*

13 Reitlinger, *page 398.*

14 *C.N., page 32.* Even Reitlinger who tends to be conservative in estimating the number of the victims admits that Ohlendorf's figures are improbably low. Reitlinger cites Ohlendorf's displeasure over the Rumanian massacres for their lack of order and thoroughness, *The Final Solution, pages 398* and *84, 201.*

15 *C.N., page 34.*

16 *Ibid., page 33.*

17 *Ibid., page 59,* Memoirs of Bernard Walter, president of the Balta Jewish Congregation.

18 *Ibid., page 93.*

19 On the question of the Jews saved by the retreating Red Army, see note below.

20 Reitlinger cites Ohlendorf's report, according to which only 551 Jews were executed. The fact is that of the 50,000 Kishinev Jews 11,252 were interned in the ghetto. What happened to the remaining nearly 30,000? No one can believe that the rapidly withdrawing Russians could have evacuated all of them. Allowing that 10,000 joined the Russians, there are still approximately 20,000 unaccounted for. There can be no doubt that the great majority of them were murdered.

21 On the eve of the German-Russian war he wrote to Hitler: " . . . I shall participate in the action to be launched in the East until the bitter end and I *set no conditions whatever,* (author's italics) and I shall discuss this military enterprise under no conditions." *P.M.T., page 18.* Even when all was lost he would not desert Hitler; he preferred to continue sacrificing masses of Rumanian youths on the battlefields, *Ibid., pages 56–58.*

22 *Ibid., page 35.*

23 Orders to issue these instructions awaited Gen. Topor upon his return from a trip to Bucharest.

Chapter 3

1 *C.N., page 92.* Circular order No. 1. The first order (No. 1) issued after the occupation of Bessarabia! In the turmoil of the newly-launched war, *this* was their great problem!

2 *Ibid., page 81.*
3 *Ibid., loc. cit.*
4 *Ibid., page 65,* Pretor of Army III, Es. II, No. 121011. The names of the mass murderers are: Cpl. Sofian Ignatz, Agafitei Gregore, Negura Vasile.
5 *Ibid., page 66.*
6 *Ibid. page 98,* Order No. 528, VIII, 8.
7 *Ibid., page 105,* Order No. 2,356, VIII, 17.
8 *Ibid., page 97,* Report of Gendarme Inspector, No. 838 VIII, 8, 1941.
9 *Ibid., page 98,* Pretor's Office, Flamura, No. 74, VIII, 8, 1941.
10 *Ibid., loc. cit.* Report of the Inspector of the Gendarmerie.
11 *Ibid., pages 113, 118.*
12 *Ibid., page 100,* No. 546–1,080 Aug. 9, 1941.
13 *Ibid., page 101,* No. 555–858 Aug. 10, 1941.
14 *Ibid., pages 114–16.*
15 *Ibid., pages 118–19,* Report No. 7,438, Sept. 11, 1941.
16 *Ibid., page 86.*
17 *Ibid., pages 120–3.*
18 *Ibid., pages 125–8,* Indictment of the People's Court.
19 *Ibid., page 126.*
20 Report of the Commission of Inquiry, *page 63.*
21 Indictment of the People's Court, *pages 120–3.*
22 *Ibid.,* No. 808, Sept. 2, 1941, *pages 116–17.*
23 *Ibid.,* No. 666, Sept. 3, 1941, *page 117.*
24 *Ibid., page 123.*
25 *Ibid., page 64, ff.* Report of the Commission of Inquiry of December, 1941.
26 *Ibid., page 87.*
27 *C.N., page 143.*
28 *Ibid., loc. cit.*
29 Reitlinger, *page 84.*
30 How typical of the self-effacement of the Rumanians, that a German should decide the fate of Rumanian citizens! The Consul showed more wisdom and dignity in refusing this role.
31 Seven months later the "Popovici Jews" were deported.
32 Mayor Popovici gave the following account of these events:

> The population marked for deportation was assembled in groups of 2,000 and driven through mud and mire to the freight depot of the railroad station. Here,

squeezed into coaches, 40–50 persons in a coach, the train was set in motion in the direction of Attachi and Marculesti. Nerve-wracking scenes took place at the departure of the trains. The separation of families with children leaving and parents remaining or vice versa; the tearing away of sisters from brothers, even husbands from wives, filled the air with wails, touching even the stoniest hearts. It was a separation forever . . .

The exodus of the Jews from Czernowitz constitutes and will everlastingly mark the deepest depravity of culture and civilization . . . Their despoliation at the Dniester, the destruction of their documents so that their traces would disappear, their marching in wind, rain, slush and mud, naked and hungry—these are pages from Dante's Inferno of apocalyptic savagery. In a single transport of 60 infants one survived . . .

And all this happened in the twentieth century.

In the name of humaneness, of civilization, of a religion teaching love, *history will spit on us.*

"With the blood of the martyrs, with the souls of those whose sufferings were superhuman, with the horror of those who went down into the valley of death, the new priests of a savage cult wrote a page of apocalyptic shame into the Psalter of the Rumanian race."

33 Reitlinger states, with reference to the Jewish Social Studies April, 1946, that the Jews in the Kishinev ghetto were saved and in 1944 were liberated by the Red Army. This statement is erroneous.

34 Here is an excerpt from the report of that Special Committee:

From the report submitted by the Inspectorate of the Gendarmerie in Kishinev it appears that at the various points of entry (Transnistria) 55,867 Jews were sent from Bessarabia and 45,538 from Bukovina.

Concerning the Bessarabian Jews there is a difference of about 25,000 Jews between the 75,000–80,000 who had been interned in the lagers and these 55,867 Jews who were deported. (These 25,000) died of natural causes or escaped or were shot to death . . .

This document clearly proves that the Kishinev ghetto

was deported to Transnistria. Otherwise in explaining the difference between the number of Jews interned and the number deported, the Commission would surely have mentioned the non-deported Kishinev ghetto.

True, on Oct. 14, 1941, the deportations from Czernowitz and Kishinev were suspended, but concerning Kishinev the order was not enforced. As late as on Oct. 29 and 31 the Chief of the Company 23 of the Bessarabian police reported the deportation of Jews—the last inmates of the Kishinev ghetto. (*C.N., page 128*) Finally in May, 1942 the Central Office of the Jews in Rumania took a "racial census of the inhabitants of Jewish blood." This was carried out with strict obedience because of the heavy penalties for infractions. According to this census at that date the number of the Jews in Bessarabia was 227. The liberation by the Red Army of 9,000 Jews in 1944 in Kishinev, therefore, seems to be a myth.

35 He refers to the cession in 1940 of Bessarabia to the Russians. He ignores the fact that his "great ally" Hitler, was responsible for the cession.

36 Reitlinger, *page 95;* A. Goldstein, *Their Mournful Road, page 11,* gives the date as Dec. 9.

37 Reitlinger, *op. cit., pages 97, 213.*

38 *Ibid., pages 20–2.*

39 Goldstein, *op. cit., page 8.*

40 Reitlinger, *op. cit., page 79;* Goldstein, *op. cit., page 8.*

41 Reitlinger, *op. cit., pages 82, 95;* Goldstein, *op. cit., page 11.*

42 Reitlinger, *op. cit., page 37, ff;* Goldstein, *op. cit., page 11.*

43 Heydrich's opening words at the Wannsee conference. Cf. Goldstein, *page 12.*

44 Reitlinger, *op. cit., pages 80–84, 390–1.*

45 *See* Goldstein: *Operation Murder, page 10* on the complicity of the Commanders of the *Reichswehr.* Also Reitlinger, *page 348* concerning Keitel's role.

46 Reitlinger, *op. cit., page 312.*

47 *Ibid., page 333.*

48 *Ibid., page 343.*

49 *Ibid., page 351.*

50 *Ibid., page 372.*

51 Despite Mussolini's regime, the Italian people and army, far from oppressing the Jews *saved* them whenever and wherever they could.

52 *C.N., page 231.*
53 *Ibid., page 244.* The following incident is characteristic
of Marinescu's methods. When his men entered the home
of the Nasch family they found there four bodies of
women who had poisoned themselves. Only an old woman
and a six-month-old child were alive. The soldiers had no
heart to seize them. Marinescu hastened to the scene.
There he saw one of the soldiers crying. "Why do you
cry?" he asked him. "Sir," answered the soldier, "I too
have two children and an old mother at home." Marinescu
punished the soldier and ordered the old woman together
with the infant deported. At another occasion a woman
with her baby on her arm ran up onto the platform
where she stood and pleaded for her life. He kicked her
in the bosom and sent her tumbling down together with
the child.
54 *Ibid., page 276.*
55 Even a Christian butcher, N. Teodoru was sent to a labor
camp for selling spoiled meat.
56 Decree 5,295 Apr. 21, 1942. Law decree No. 503—1942.
57 Characteristic of his venom is this episode. A group of
Czernowitz Jews worked on a road near Piatra Neamtz.
The general in the disguise of a country squire off to the
hunt, sneaked among them to spy upon their behavior.
After a recess 25 Jews were somewhat late in reporting to
work. The general identified them and had them deported
to Transnistria.
58 Reitlinger, *pages 403, 404.*
59 On the basis of personal experience with the Metropolit,
this author thinks that this version is the correct one.
60 *C.N., pages 237-8.*

Chapter 4

1 Report of Jan. 15, 1944, for the Rumanian Social Institute,
page 320.
2 Here are their names: Drs. A. Reicher, F. Siegel, A. Koch,
S. Kraemer, S. Schaechter, I. Schieber, A. Hermann, J.
Wucher, B. Harth, J. Kerth, H. Holdengraeber, S.
Schnarch.
3 *C.N., page 447.*

4 *Ibid., page 290.*
5 *Ibid., page 363.*
6 Reitlinger, *pages 236, 241.*
7 *C.N., page 285.*
8 *Ibid., page 369.*

Chapter 5

1 *C.N., page 320.*
2 Among them were: Herman Dolfig and his wife, M. Heinig and his wife, the aged Mrs. Kerzner. *Ibid., page 261.*
3 This number is based on Report No. 42,411 of the General Superintendent of the Rumanian Gendarmerie, Sept. 1, 1943. According to it the number of the Jews in these settlements was reduced by half during the first two years. In Sept. 1943 their number was 19,166; thus their original number must have been about 40,000. *Ibid., page 440.*
4 Jaegendorf's report, *Ibid., page 362.*
5 *Ibid., page 384.*
6 Report prepared for the Rumanian Social Institute, Bucharest.
7 Doctors A. Reicher, F. Siegel, A. Koch, S. Kraemer, S. Schaechter, I. Schieber, A. Hermann, I. Wucher, B. Harth, J. Kerth, H. Holdengraeber, S. Schnarch, died in the field of duty.
8 *C.N., pages 337 ff.*
9 Reitlinger, *pages 195 ff.*
10 *Ibid., page 269.*
11 *C.N., pages 357–8.* The figure of 20,000 cannot be taken at its face value. He most probably refers to the 24,000 Bessarabian Jews who, before the conclusion of the German-Rumanian agreement establishing Transnistria, were driven to Moghilev and from there returned to Bessarabia. Several thousands of them were destroyed by the Germans.
12 *Ibid., page 368.*

Chapter 6

1 *Hitler's Ten Year War on the Jews, page 202.*
2 *Ibid., page 186.*
3 Reitlinger, *page 227 ff., page 399.*

4 Treatment of the Jews under Communism, Special Report No. 2, House Report No. 2684, Part 5, f *15 ff.*
5 According to Reitlinger, *op. cit., page 240,* Ohlendorf's men might have planted the mine.
6 *Ibid., loc. cit.*
7 *P.M.T., page 287, ff.*
8 *Ibid.*
9 *Ibid., 298 ff.*
10 *Ibid., loc. cit.*
11 *Ibid., loc. cit.*
12 Report No. 76, Jan. 17, 1942.
13 *C.N., pages 202–6.*
14 *Ibid., pages 226–7.*
15 It is amazing that such a profound student of this period as Mr. Reitlinger could make so gross a misstatement. In his *op. cit., page 240,* he states: "No attempt was made to exterminate the remaining Jews in Odessa (after the massacre of Oct. 23–24). It seems . . . that the Jews were distributed among the Transnistrian towns with the deportees from Rumania . . . a number were deliberately brought back to Odessa in May, 1942." He bases his assumption on Brautigam's report of May 23, 1942, "which said that a large portion of the Jews in Transnistria died, the others were transported to Odessa." *(Ibid., page 402).* Of course, they were transported to Odessa according to Decree No. 7. But this was not the end of their story as Reitlinger optimistically assumes. From Odessa they were shipped North to their death by the *Einsatz* henchmen. Reitlinger is unaware of this as he has not seen the long series of the police-reports on the plight and end of these Jews.

Unfortunately, this is not the only misstatement in the book of this respected scholar.

Chapter 7

1 *P.M.T., page 163.*
2 A few days before Germany's surrender Himmler released 1,000 Hungarian Jewish girls from the concentration camps. Reitlinger, *page 241.*

Chapter 8

1 According to the census, the number of Jews in Greater Rumania (including the Old Kingdom, all of Transylvania and Bukovina and the provinces of Bessarabia and Dobruja) was 756,930. This figure was challenged by the Rumanian fascists who, for propaganda purposes, asserted that this population actually numbered between two to three million. In 1941 the Rumanian Government invited F. Burgdorfer, president of the Bavarian Office of Statistics, to decide the question; he upheld the accuracy of the 1930 census. Cf. A.E., page 8

2 This census held prior to the outbreak of war with Russia, does not include the territories which had been ceded to neighboring countries on Apr. 6, 1941—North Transylvania to Hungary, North Bukovina and Bessarabia to Soviet Russia, Dobruja to Bulgaria. We are primarily interested in these ceded territories for which no 1941 statistics were prepared. Extrapolation of 1930 data is required to obtain statistics for 1941. C.N. assumes that this population declined during the decade 1930–40. The examination of 1941 data for unceded territories refutes this contention and indicates that the number of non-deported Jews declined. [Cf. P.E. (note 4 below) page 24, A.E., pages 19–20.] Thus the data from 1930 can be relied upon for the ceded territories.

3 This census can be assumed to be reliable. The Central Office of Rumanian Jews was ordered, under threat of penalty for error, to make an accurate tabulation. (Cf. C.N., page 41, n.1). On Sept. 1, 1941, the third month of the war, the Rumanian Office of Statistics conducted a census, "The Inventory of the Jewish Population of the Recovered Territories." Prepared at the time of the deportations, its data are of doubtful value. (Ibid.). However, to remain conservative, some of its statistics were taken into consideration.

4 P.E., page 52. The figure 301,886 is the sum of the number of Jews in the territories annexed to Russia (277,949) (North Bukovina and Bessarabia) and the number of Jews in South Bukovina (23,937). (Ibid.).

5 C.N., pages 41–2; Census of May 20, 1942; P.E., page 54.

6 Report prepared by Gen. Topor on instructions of the General Headquarters of the Rumanian Army (Sept. 4, 1941), (Cf. C.N., pages 117–18). Report of the Inspectorate of Gendarmerie of Bessarabia (Intr. 721. Aug. 31, 1941) and Report of the Inspectorate of Gendarmerie of Czernowitz (Intr. 925. Sept. 16, 1941). (C.N., pages 114–16). According to the latter, the number of inmates might have been 2,923 less, but we accepted the larger, in this case more conservative, figure. The original number of the inmates was considerably larger. There were about 8,000 deaths among the group of 20–25,000 driven (July 25, 1941) from Coshlar, Bessarabia to Transnistria and after weeks of aimless wandering, driven back on Aug. 11. (C.N., pages 82–3). The "Report on Investigation No. 2 of the Commission Established in Accordance with the Order of Marshal Ion Antonescu, the Leader of the State, in Order to Investigate the Irregularities in the Ghetto of Kishinev" (Dec. 1941) states clearly that concerning the Jews of Bessarabia there is a difference of 25,000 Jews "who died of natural causes, escaped or were shot to death by methods to be shown further below." (C.N., page 61).

7 The sources for the number of the Jews in the Kishinev ghetto are: Report prepared by General Topor (see note 6), C.N., page 118. P.E., page 38; Report of Ion Antonescu to the Council of Ministers, Oct. 6, 1941 (C.N., page 143). The deportation of this ghetto is reported by the Inspectorate of the Gendarmerie of Kishinev (No. 57, Oct. 29, 1941; No. 61, Oct. 31, 1941. (C.N., page 128). Reitlinger, page 398, cites the study by Leon Shapiro and Joshua Starr, "Recent Population Data Regarding the Jews in Europe," Jewish Social Studies, vol. viii (1946), pages 75–80, to the effect that the Jews in Kishinev were saved and liberated in 1944 by the Red Army. However, the statement cited by Reitlinger from the study by Shapiro and Starr is non-existent. The "Report of the Commission to Investigate Irregularities in the Ghetto of Kishinev" states: "From the report submitted by the Inspectorate of the Gendarmerie in Kishinev, it appears that at the various points of entry (to Transnistria) 55,867 Jews were sent from Bessarabia and 45,538 from Bukovina. Concerning the Bessarabian Jews there is a difference of about 25,000 Jews between the 75–80,000 Jews interned in the camps and between those who were deported. These

25,000 died of natural causes or escaped or were shot to death." These sentences prove that by Dec. 1941 the ghetto inmates had already been deported. Otherwise, the explanation might have read: "Of these 25,000, 10,000 are still in the Kishinev ghetto, while 15,000 died . . . " The fact that no mention is made of the Kishinev ghetto indicates it no longer existed. To be sure, deportations from Czernowitz and Kishinev were suspended on Oct. 14, 1941, but, as far as Kishinev was concerned, this was not enforced. As late as Oct. 29 and 31, the chief of Company 23 of the Bessarabian Police reported the deportation of 1,004 Jews, *C.N., page 120.* On May 20, 1942, the Central Office of the Jews of Rumania carried out a "Racial Census" (*cf.* above *n. 3*). It revealed that all in all 99 Jews lived in "the territories incorporated by Soviet Russia," *P.E., page 52.* Therefore, "the reported liberation of 9,000 Jews by the Red Army in 1944" appears to us to be a myth.

8 The Jewish population was 51,681 (1930 Census). The "Inventory" of September 1941, found there 49,497 Jews, *C.N., page 42.*

9 *C.N., pages 139, 143, 176.*

10 *C.N., pages 133, 137, 143.*

11 *C.N., page 42* on the basis of the April 1941 Census, and *page 137* on the fact that 170 were not deported.

12 *Ibid., page 42.*

13 *Ibid., pages 231–33.*

14 From Targu-Jiu, 407; from jails, 85; and from other places, 554, *C.N., page 450.*

15 Of these, 594 were deported for infractions of the forced labor laws, and 578 for having opted for the Soviet Union. (*Ibid.*)

16 *Ibid., page 38.*

17 Report No. 42,411, Sept. 16, 1943, *C.N., pages 436–42.*

18 *Ibid., page 409.*

19 *Ibid., pages 442, 450.*

20 This figure is shown in the report of the Ministry of Internal Affairs based on the report of the Gendarmerie Inspectorate of Sept. 16, 1943 *C.N., page 450.* At the end of April of the same year, 427 Jews were released from Vapniarka to the Transnistrian towns of Olgopol, Savrani, and Tridubi. (Report of the Inspector General of Gendarmerie to the Minister of Internal Affairs, May 1, 1943, *C.N., pages 428–29*).

21 The Gendarmerie's report puts the number of "evacuees" at 99,798. It uses the data of the Kishinev Investigating Commission, but arbitrarily reduces the number of Bukovina deportees from 45,332 to 43,798. The report of the Ministry of Internal Affairs adds to this 10,368 deportees from the Dorohoi Department, thus arriving at a total of 110,033. The superficiality of these reports, however, is conspicuous. Both omit the 1942 deportations (except from Dorohoi). Yet, even the Ministry concedes that half of their number, 59,292, died.

22 *Tradare, pages 284–88.*

23 Modest Isopescu, prefect of Golta Department, hardly known outside Rumania, was almost as unknown within the country. It was this monster who destroyed in these three places about 70,000 Jews in a most horrible manner. (PMT, *pages 298–300, Scanteia,* Bucharest, May 21, 1945, Summation of Chief Prosecutor, H. Bunaciu.

24 *CN, pages 226–27* report of the Rumanian Gendarmerie.

25 *CN, page 286.*

26 *Ibid., pages 285–6.*

27 *Ibid., page 282.*

28 *Ibid., page 284.*

29 *Ibid., pages 285, 288, 294.*

30 *Ibid., page 295.*

31 *Ibid., page 300.*

32 Diary of Moses Katz, former president of Moghilev and Scazinetz, *Ibid., page 357.*

33 *See* Joseph B. Shechtman, *The Transnistria Reservation.*

Bibliography

Abbreviations used in notes, in alphabetical order:

A.E.—Asezarile Evreilor din Romania (The Settlement of the Jews in Rumania).
C.N.—Cartea Neagra (The Black Book).
Gheorghe—Rumaniens Weg Zum Satellitenstaat, Ion Gheorghe.
Hillgruber—Hitler, König Carol and Marschall Antonescu, Andreas Hillgruber.
P.E.—Populatia Evreeasca in Cifre (The Jewish Population in Figures).
P.M.T.—Procesul Marii Tradari Nationale (The Trial of the Great National Betrayal).
Reitlinger—The Final Solution, Gerald Reitlinger.

Note: The above sources will be identified more fully in the bibliographical listing that follows:

Books

Carp, Matatias, ed. *Cartea Neagra; Fapte si Documente, Suferintele Evreilor din Romania, 1940-44* (The Black Book; Facts and Documents, The Sufferings of the Jews of Rumania, 1940-1944). Vol. 3, Transnistria. Bucharest, 1947.
This is the basic source for this period. Unfortunately, its day-by-day method disrupts and atomizes the events, making them difficult, and at times impossible, to follow. Its greatest merit is its rich documentation, upon which we chiefly relied.

Reitlinger, Gerald. *The Final Solution*. New York. A. S. Barnes, 1953.

This is a monument of erudition. Unfortunately, however, the Rumanian sources do not seem to have been accessible to the author. This handicap plus his unfounded optimism misled him into a gross underestimation of the number of victims and into other errors of fact. I felt in duty bound to take issue with him wherever he deviates from clearly proven facts.

Documents

Procesul Marii Tradari Nationale: Stenograma Desbaterilor dela Tribunalul Popurului asupra Guvernului Antonescu (The Trial of the Great National Betrayal: The Stenographic Record of the Antonescue Government Trial Before the People's Tribunal). Bucharest, 1946.

United States Department of State. 1946-48. *Nazi Conspiracy and Aggression*. Washington, D.C.

World Jewish Congress. 1943. *Hitler's Ten-Year War on the Jews*. New York: Institute of Jewish Affairs.

————. 1945. *Populatia Evreeasca in Cifre* (The Jewish Population in Figures). Bucharest.

————. 1947. *Asezarile Evreilor din Romania* (The Settlement of the Jews in Rumania. Bucharest.

————. 1948. *Unity in Dispersion*. New York.

On the historical background:

Books

Elbogen. Ismar. *A Century of Jewish Life*. Philadelphia: The Jewish Publication Society of America, 1946.

Gafencu, Grigore. *Vorspiel zum Krieg in Osten* (Prelude to the Russian Campaign).

————. *Europas Letzte Tage* (Last Days of Europe). Zurich, 1948.

Gheorghe, Ion. *Rumaniens Weg Zum Satellitenstaat.* Heidelberg, 1952.

Hillgruber, Andreas. *Hitler, König Carol and Marschall Antonescu:* Die Deutch-Rumanischen Beziehungen, 1938-1944. Wiesbaden: F. Steiner, 1954.

Schellenberg, Walter. *Hitler's Secret Service.* Translated and edited by Louis Hagen. New York: Pyramid Books, 1958.

Documents

Government Press. 1943. *Trei Ani de Guvernare.* Bucharest.

United Rumanian Jews of America, 1942. *Bloodbath in Rumania,* "The Record," Vol. 4. New York.

Pamphlets

Anatole Goldstein. *Operation Murder.* World Jewish Congress, Institute of Jewish Affairs. New York, 1949.

————. *Their Mournful Road.* World Jewish Congress, Institute of Jewish Affairs. New York, 1948.

Articles

Bucharest newspaper reports on the trials of the fascist criminals.

Schechtman, Joseph B. *The Transnistria Reservation.* YIVO Annual of Jewish Social Science, Vol. 7. New York: 1953.

Index

157